Samuel French Acting Edition

Off Off Broadway Festival Plays
17th Series

Correct Address
by Judd Silverman

Cowboys, Indians & Waitresses
by Raymond King Shurtz

Homebound
by Lyndall Callahan

The Road to Nineveh
by Le Wilhelm

Your Life is a Feature Film
by Alan Minieri

SAMUELFRENCH.COM   SAMUELFRENCH.CO.UK

The Road to Niniveh © 1993 by Le Wilhelm
Correct Address © 1993 by Judd Lear Silverman
Cowboys, Indians & Waitresses © 1993 by Raymond King Shurtz
Homebound © 1993 by Lyndall Callan
Your Life is a Feature Film © 1991, 1993 by Alan Minieri
All Rights Reserved

OFF OFF BROADWAY FESTIVAL PLAYS: 17TH SERIES is fully protected under the copyright laws of the United States of America, the British Commonwealth, including Canada, and all other countries of the Copyright Union. All rights, including professional and amateur stage productions, recitation, lecturing, public reading, motion picture, radio broadcasting, television and the rights of translation into foreign languages are strictly reserved.

ISBN 978-0-573-69393-9

www.SamuelFrench.com
www.SamuelFrench.co.uk

FOR PRODUCTION ENQUIRIES

UNITED STATES AND CANADA
Info@SamuelFrench.com
1-866-598-8449

UNITED KINGDOM AND EUROPE
Plays@SamuelFrench.co.uk
020-7255-4302

Each title is subject to availability from Samuel French, depending upon country of performance. Please be aware that *OFF OFF BROADWAY FESTIVAL PLAYS: 17TH SERIES* may not be licensed by Samuel French in your territory. Professional and amateur producers should contact the nearest Samuel French office or licensing partner to verify availability.

CAUTION: Professional and amateur producers are hereby warned that *OFF OFF BROADWAY FESTIVAL PLAYS: 17TH SERIES* is subject to a licensing fee. Publication of this play(s) does not imply availability for performance. Both amateurs and professionals considering a production are strongly advised to apply to Samuel French before starting rehearsals, advertising, or booking a theatre. A licensing fee must be paid whether the title(s) is presented for charity or gain and whether or not admission is charged. Professional/Stock licensing fees are quoted upon application to Samuel French.

No one shall make any changes in this title(s) for the purpose of production. No part of this book may be reproduced, stored in a retrieval system, or transmitted in any form, by any means, now known or yet to be invented, including mechanical, electronic, photocopying, recording, videotaping, or otherwise, without the prior written permission of the publisher. No one shall upload this title(s), or part of this title(s), to any social media websites.

For all enquiries regarding motion picture, television, and other media rights, please contact Samuel French.

MUSIC USE NOTE

Licensees are solely responsible for obtaining formal written permission from copyright owners to use copyrighted music in the performance of this play and are strongly cautioned to do so. If no such permission is obtained by the licensee, then the licensee must use only original music that the licensee owns and controls. Licensees are solely responsible and liable for all music clearances and shall indemnify the copyright owners of the play(s) and their licensing agent, Samuel French, against any costs, expenses, losses and liabilities arising from the use of music by licensees. Please contact the appropriate music licensing authority in your territory for the rights to any incidental music.

IMPORTANT BILLING AND CREDIT REQUIREMENTS

If you have obtained performance rights to this title, please refer to your licensing agreement for important billing and credit requirements.

THE ROAD TO NINEVEH

by Le Wilhelm

The Road to Nineveh was presented by Love Creek Productions. It was directed by Jeffrey J. Albright and had the following cast:

HOWARD LEE ....Christian Beaird
BEVERLY ....Bridget Polk
BREEN..James Robert Robinson

The play was originally directed by Mr. Albright with the following cast:

HOWARD LEE..Ron Hirt
BEVERLY ....Merry Beamer
BREEN ....George Cron

CHARACTERS

HOWARD LEE: Manager/cook of a restaurant in Tarsus, Tennessee.

BEVERLY: A neighbor and frequent visitor at the restaurant.

BREEN: A customer at the restaurant.

TIME & PLACE

Tennessee.
Christmas Eve. The Present.

This play is dedicated to Dr. Leslie Irene Coger

We are in a restaurant. It is probably only necessary to have a couple of tables with chairs to indicate this. There are some Christmas decorations and a tree. It should not be overly decorated. At one of the tables, the manager/cook, etc., HOWARD LEE, is sitting. He is a man around thirty-five. He is a good man. He is a country man. On the radio, the ANNOUNCER says, as the LIGHTS come up, "This is WKJR in Jerusalem, Tennessee. And now I'd like to play you... (an appropriate Yuletide song). From what I can see out my window, everyone here who's been dreaming of a white Christmas certainly got their dreams fulfilled. Mother Nature is covering all of the midwest from Kansas to Tennessee with a blanket of white." Singer comes on singing... (Previously mentioned song). HOWARD LEE sits at a table and plays checkers with himself. This provides quite an emotional roller coaster, because HE's always winning and always losing.

HOWARD LEE. Got you. (*Jumping some men.*) No, you don't. (*The other side jumps and goes to the end of the board.*) Crown me. (*HE does.*) Crown me. (*HE sits and looks a moment, the other side.*) Hurry up. (*A moment passes.*) Don't rush me.

(*BEVERLY enters. She is a woman in her mid-to-late thirties, pretty.*)
BEVERLY. What're you doing, Howard Lee?

HOWARD LEE. What's it look like I'm doing, Beverly? I'm playing checkers.

BEVERLY. Who's winning?

HOWARD LEE. I am.

BEVERLY. Way to go, Howard Lee. Way to go.

HOWARD LEE. Could I get you something?

BEVERLY. Cup'a coffee.

HOWARD LEE. (*Getting up.*) Just made a pot.

BEVERLY. In that case, put it in one of them mugs. I got chilled through to the bone, walking over here.

HOWARD LEE. (*Off.*) Temperature drops much more, folks'll be getting frostbite.

BEVERLY. (*At window.*) Sure coming down.

HOWARD LEE. Weatherman said we might get up to fifteen inches.

BEVERLY. No doubt about it, it'll be a white Christmas this year.

HOWARD LEE. (*Entering with coffee.*) Be a white 'n' alright. (*Indicating cream pitcher.*) That's real cream, Beverly.

BEVERLY. Real cream?

HOWARD LEE. Un-hun.

BEVERLY. It's been ages since I've had cream in my coffee. Once in a while half and half.

HOWARD LEE. I keep it for the French Rabbit. Whenever he comes through in his eighteen wheeler, he throws a fit if I don't have real cream.

BEVERLY. (*Sipping.*) I'd forgotten how good it tastes.

HOWARD LEE. Good night for treating yourself special.

BEVERLY. Yeah. (*Changing the subject.*) Been any accidents reported?

HOWARD LEE. I got the C.B. on in the back, but no one's out tonight.

BEVERLY. Didn't you hear Larry Short on it about an hour ago?

HOWARD LEE. I heard him.

BEVERLY. Does that every year.

HOWARD LEE. C.B. Santa. I think he's crazy as a loon.

BEVERLY. Larry Short? Howard Lee, you don't need to think on it. He's a card carrying nut. Always was.

HOWARD LEE. You used to date him, didn't you?

BEVERLY. In high school.

HOWARD LEE. I remember the two of you riding around in that old beat up convertible of his.

BEVERLY. Cadillac convertible. It wasn't that beat up. Cherry red Cadillac convertible.

HOWARD LEE. It was missing a front fender, wasn't it?

BEVERLY. Yeah, but the rest of it was in good shape. I probably should have married him ... he asked. He probably wasn't serious, though.

HOWARD LEE. He thought a lot of you.

BEVERLY. Yeah, after I turned him down, it wasn't six months 'til he was engaged to Glinda.

HOWARD LEE. Six months can be a long time.

BEVERLY. Yeah, it can. I probably should have married him ... but I had to go shopping around ... had to go all the way to Atlanta to find the right one ... and look what I brung home.

HOWARD LEE. Ain't heard from him?

BEVERLY. No. Don't reckon I'm going to.

HOWARD LEE. Never know.

BEVERLY. He didn't even say goodbye. Just left. I'll never hear from him. (*A moment.*) Quite a snowstorm. Ain't it?

HOWARD LEE. Kids are tickled to death over it. But it's a bad one. Going to do some damage. Power lines are down in a lot of places.

BEVERLY. I heard on the radio that in the northern part of the state, it's real bad. I guess the entire town of Bethlehem is without light.

HOWARD LEE. That's what they're reporting.

BEVERLY. Odd, ain't it?

HOWARD LEE. What?

BEVERLY. Bethlehem without lights on Christmas Eve.

HOWARD LEE. Mmh.

BEVERLY. You know, Howard, I bet between southern Missouri, Arkansas, Tennessee and Kentucky, there ain't a city in the Bible that's not got one named after it.

HOWARD LEE. May be right.

BEVERLY. Here we are in Tarsus. That's where Saul—

HOWARD LEE. I don't recall any places called Sodom or Gomorrah.

BEVERLY. No ... but they wouldn't, would they? Larry's probably better off marrying Glinda.

HOWARD LEE. What?

BEVERLY. I said Larry Short is probably better off with Glinda.

HOWARD LEE. You like a warm up?

BEVERLY. Mmh. I can get it.

HOWARD LEE. No, let me. I ain't done anything all

day 'cept play checkers and—

BEVERLY. He's got a nice family ... all them kids ... and I like Glinda. (*Noticing the checkerboard.*) Crazy you being open tonight.

HOWARD LEE. (*Off.*) Do what the boss says.

BEVERLY. I know, but it's silly ... ain't nobody here but me.

HOWARD LEE. Surprised to see you tonight, Bev.

BEVERLY. Didn't have anything better—

HOWARD LEE. I figured you'd go over to Leo and Anna's.

BEVERLY. They asked.

HOWARD LEE. Should have gone.

BEVERLY. Aah.

HOWARD LEE. You should have.

BEVERLY. Howard Lee, it ain't much fun being the third person out. It's like three on a match ... if you know what I mean.

HOWARD LEE. They'd've enjoyed—

BEVERLY. Maybe ... but they're not family ... I ain't got a family ... all buried ... and I ain't got a husband ... he ran off and left me ... oh, they say they want me to come over ... but Christmas is a time for family ... if you're not family, you're not really wanted ... it's just an obligation—

HOWARD LEE. I don't think you're right about—

BEVERLY. It's something you don't understand. You're married. You got a family. I'm different.

HOWARD LEE. I guess.

BEVERLY. It just don't make good business sense, them making you keep this place open on Christmas Eve.

HOWARD LEE. They leave it up to the individual

managers. We can either work on Christmas or Christmas Eve. Mary Ann said there was no way she'd let me work on Christmas Day. 'Sides, I only have to keep it open to midnight.

BEVERLY. Still it's—

HOWARD LEE. Sometimes it's better off not to argue about things.

BEVERLY. I 'spect so.

HOWARD LEE. Un-hun.

BEVERLY. 'Spect I never really learned that lesson, though. When Mom and Dad were alive, we always passed our presents out on Christmas Eve.

HOWARD LEE. So do we. Mary Ann puts everyone to bed early, then she gets out the gifts and, when I get home at midnight, we get them out of bed and have our Christmas Eve ... then we sleep late.

BEVERLY. I can't believe you can get the kids to sleep ...

HOWARD LEE. They probably play possum ... but the girls love it.

BEVERLY. You've got yourself two pretty little girls.

HOWARD LEE. I think so. Beverly, would you like to come over for Christmas dinner—We'd all—

BEVERLY. No.

HOWARD LEE. You sure?

BEVERLY. I'm sure.

HOWARD LEE. I worry about you.

BEVERLY. I'm fine.

HOWARD LEE. Mary Ann's an awful good cook.

BEVERLY. I know she is. But you see ...

(There is a pause.)

HOWARD LEE. What?

BEVERLY. Well, I got a houseful of food. Howard Lee, I just went a little crazy yesterday.

HOWARD LEE. No, you didn't.

BEVERLY. Yes, I did. I just went a little crazy. I just started cooking like a house afire. Fixing everything I like. I got a sugar cured ham, and I went to the grocery and I bought all the fresh green beans they had. I just love green beans. Always have, even when I's a young'n'. I fixed everything I like ... three bean salad, green bean casserole ... I got enough cooked up at home to feed an army, Howard Lee. Me living alone.

HOWARD LEE. You ain't got company coming?

BEVERLY. No. I just went a little crazy.

HOWARD LEE. If you like cooking ... most things'll keep.

BEVERLY. And I got a great big tree. Cut it down myself over on the Delk Place, and I strung it with popcorn and cranberries like I did when I was a kid ... got out all the old ornaments ...

HOWARD LEE.. We strung popcorn this year, too— Mary Ann and the kids dyed it pink and blue.

BEVERLY. I bet that's pretty.

HOWARD LEE. Oh, it is. You'll have to come over and take a gander at it before we take it down.

BEVERLY. And then, Howard, I even went out and I bought presents. I bought a present for myself ... and ... and I bought one for Bob. I guess it was for Bob ... I didn't actually write his name on it ... I did that just on the off chance he might show up ... it's a beautiful tree, Howard. And I made a strawberry chiffon pie, and a sour cream chocolate cake ... and I made them all from scratch, no mixes. Cookies in the shape of little Santas and trees ... with candy sparkles on them ... but he ain't coming back. I know that.

HOWARD LEE. He might.

BEVERLY. No, he won't. And if he did, I'd meet him at the door with a shotgun and tell him that he had to the count of three to get off my property. *(Laughing.)*

HOWARD LEE. He'd deserve that, Beverly.

BEVERLY. It's crazy, but I always thought it would work. You see, Bob liked green beans as much as I did.

HOWARD LEE. A lot of people like beans, Bev.

BEVERLY. No, he was crazy about them. And I was crazy to fix all that food and ... well, but I've always been a little crazy.

HOWARD LEE. No, you haven't.

BEVERLY. Yes, I have. Like the beans. How many little kids do you know that love beans? But I was so crazy about them that I'd put them in my nose and in my ears. Momma always said one of them was going to get caught and sprout. *(SHE laughs.)* You wouldn't like to play a game of checkers, would you?

HOWARD LEE. Sure. But I have to warn you, I'm the defending champion. I buried the last person I played. Poor guy didn't stand a chance.

BEVERLY. Red or black?

HOWARD LEE. You pick.

(BREEN "SPOONBILL" enters. HE is a man around their age. HE is very cold, having been walking for some time in the storm. HE should have a degree of charisma, although HE need not be strikingly

handsome, HE certainly should have a certain allure about him.)

BEVERLY. *(Starting.)* Oh, my God!! Where'd you—
BREEN. I slid off—
HOWARD LEE. Here, let me help—
BEVERLY. He's nearly frozen to death—
BREEN. I'm alright.
HOWARD LEE. I'll get some coffee.
BEVERLY. Just keep walking for a while. Are your feet alright?
BREEN. Yeah.
BEVERLY. They're not numb?
BREEN. No.
BEVERLY. You sure?
BREEN. They're fine.
BEVERLY. Why don't you take off your gloves?
HOWARD LEE. *(With coffee.)* Here we go.
BREEN. Thanks. *(Taking coffee, drinking.)* Ouch.
BEVERLY. Not so fast—
HOWARD LEE. Plenty more where that came from.
BREEN. I got to get the car out—
BEVERLY. What did you do, slide off the road?
BREEN. Yeah. I got to get it out and get back on the road.
HOWARD LEE. Whoa—you ain't going nowhere.
BREEN. I got to—
BEVERLY. The roads are all closed—No one'll be travelling 'til late tomorrow.
BREEN. I got to. I got to get to Niniveh.
HOWARD LEE. Niniveh?
BREEN. This is the road to Niniveh, isn't it?

BEVERLY. Niniveh, Arkansas?

BREEN. Yeah.

BEVERLY. This is the right road, but it's over a hundred miles away; you'll never get there.

BREEN. I got to.

HOWARD LEE. You might "got to" mister, but there's no way you will tonight.

BREEN. Isn't there a garage around that could pull me—

HOWARD LEE. This is Christmas Eve. Ain't no one around here working, 'cept me.

BREEN. I got to find a way.

HOWARD LEE. Not going to in this storm.

BEVERLY. You got folks in Niniveh?

BREEN. Sort of.

BEVERLY. They'll understand. They wouldn't want you out in this storm.

BREEN. It's not like that. I was born there ... I haven't been back—(*HE is shaking.*)

BEVERLY. Howard Lee, get him some more coffee and bring him some soup. He's chilled clean through to the bone.

BREEN. Thanks.

BEVERLY. You just take it easy.

BREEN. Yeah.

BEVERLY. My name's Beverly, or Bev. What's yours?

BREEN. Breen.

BEVERLY. Breen. That's an unusual one.

BREEN. Everyone calls me Spoonbill.

BEVERLY. Spoonbill?

BREEN. Yeah, after the catfish. Spoonbill catfish.

BEVERLY. What did you do, catch a big one once?

BREEN. When I was growing up. I was fishing in a little creek that runs into the Mississippi, and I caught this fish. It was after a flood, and I guess he was trapped in the hole of water—but he weighed almost a hundred pounds.

BEVERLY. Shhs—how'd a kid land a fish that big?

BREEN. Took most of the day.

BEVERLY. I'd imagine.

BREEN. (*Looks out the window.*) Darn, how long's this supposed to keep up.

BEVERLY. All night. Spoonbill, you might as well forget making it to Niniveh. No way in this weather.

BREEN. Darn, just darn it!! Of all the dang blasted things—

BEVERLY. I'm sorry, I know folks like to be with their families.

BREEN. Just my gol blasted luck!! Heck fire!

BEVERLY. (*Laughs.*) I'm sorry.

BREEN. It's not funny.

BEVERLY. I know. I just ... no offense, but I've never heard a man curse quite like you do.

BREEN. Well, I don't usually. You see, my momma just hated cussing, and when she was dying, she made me promise not to cuss on Good Friday, Easter, Christmas and Christmas Eve and her birthday. I do my best to grant her dying wish—Sometimes I f—, mess up, but I try.

BEVERLY. That's nice of you.

BREEN. Least a son can do is try to respect his ma's dying wish.

BEVERLY. I guess that's so.

HOWARD LEE. (*Entering with a bowl of soup.*) You doing better?

BREEN. Yeah.

HOWARD LEE. This'll warm you up.

BREEN. Thanks. I'm feeling better.

HOWARD LEE. You know, the phones are still working, and if you'd like you can use the private phone.

BREEN. (*Eating.*) What for?

HOWARD LEE. To call. To call your family in Niniveh.

BREEN. Oh, no I couldn't do that.

HOWARD LEE. I don't care. You could call collect or have the operator call with the charges.

BREEN. No, you don't understand.

BEVERLY. Don't your family have a phone?

BREEN. I don't have a family there. They're all dead.

BEVERLY. Then why are you so anxious to—

BREEN. The house is still there. I keep it—

BEVERLY. Your brothers and sisters come in from all over—?

BREEN. No, there's no one. I'm alone now.

HOWARD LEE. No one?

BREEN. No. But I go home at Christmas. Be there with the ghosts.

BEVERLY. You see ghosts?

BREEN. No. Not real ghosts. The memories. I'm ... you see I didn't make it home for a while. I ... I had friends and ... didn't have enough money to make it back or didn't want to spend the ... it's not a good thing ... there are certain obligations I failed to meet, I'm afraid ... and when I decided to meet them, wanted to ... because ... because I needed to .... they're gone. And so I go back for the memories—Bittersweet to say the least.

BEVERLY. Sounds lonely.

BREEN. Believe it or not, it's about the only time I'm not lonely. Howard Lee?

HOWARD LEE. Yeah.

BREEN. You make one good bowl of soup.

HOWARD LEE. Thanks.

BEVERLY. Howard Lee, don't you take credit for that. You know very well Betty makes the soup.

HOWARD LEE. Yeah, she does.

BREEN. Well, you tell Betty a stranger came through, and he loved her soup.

(Offstage, we hear a FEMALE VOICE on the C.B.: "Break. Break for Donald Duck.")

HOWARD LEE. That's for me. It's Mary Ann. I'd better see what she wants.

(HOWARD LEE exits as FEMALE VOICE continues to break.)

BEVERLY. So what are you going to do now? You can't make it to—

BREEN. I got to figure out a way.

HOWARD LEE. *(Off.)* You got Donald Duck. Is that the Daisy?

(At this, a door is shut and we only hear the VOICE MUFFLED.)

BEVERLY. Even if you could make it to the state line, the bridge across the Mississippi is iced over. Completely closed down.

BREEN. Goin' to be a bad year if I don't make it to Niniveh for Christmas.

BEVERLY. You'll make it. You'll just be a little late.

HOWARD LEE. (*Entering.*) Beverly, Mary Ann's having trouble getting the girls' bicycles out of the attic. I wonder if you two would mind watching the store while I go help. I wouldn't ask you, but she has to wrap the things up. I never heard of anything so silly as wrapping bicycles ...

BEVERLY. Sure, you go ahead. We'll be fine.

HOWARD LEE. You sure you don't—

BEVERLY. Not at all, just go on.

HOWARD LEE. Okay, I'll be back in a jiffy. (*HOWARD LEE exits.*)

BEVERLY. Could you use a splash more java?

BREEN. Yeah. Thanks.

BEVERLY. You know, that's real cream.

BREEN. I noticed. I'd forgotten how good it tastes.

(*SHE refills his coffee.*)

BREEN. It being Christmas Eve, I'm surprised you're not with your family.

BEVERLY. Are you?

BREEN. You don't appear to work here.

BEVERLY. No. No, I don't.

BREEN. I didn't think you did.

BEVERLY. I live close by.

BREEN. I see.

BEVERLY. You can see the lights of my house through the window. Right over there. See.

BREEN. Yeah. Two story house.

BEVERLY. Two and a half.
BREEN. Cream is good in coffee.
BEVERLY. It is, isn't it?
BREEN. Un-hun.
BEVERLY. No. I'm like you, Spoonbill. I don't got no family. I'm an orphan, too.
BREEN. Really.
BEVERLY. Un-hun.
BREEN. Not many people that don't have a family of some sort.
BEVERLY. Oh, I got some distant cousins.
BREEN. So do I.
BEVERLY. There's one difference between you and I, Spoonbill.
BREEN. Yeah?
BEVERLY. I'm not wearing a wedding ring.
BREEN. Oh, this.
BEVERLY. Yeah, that.
BREEN. I forget about it sometimes.
BEVERLY. I can see that you do. And that ring makes a powerful lot of difference between you and me.
BREEN. It's there for a reason.
BEVERLY. They usually are.
BREEN. It reminds me that when you deal in reality to watch your step.
BEVERLY. I see.
BREEN. Do you?
BEVERLY. Would you like to play a game of checkers?
BREEN. Do you play a lot?
BEVERLY. Once in a while. I'm not any good.
BREEN. I wouldn't be a challenge for you. I haven't

played in ages.
BEVERLY. What does it matter?
BREEN. I wouldn't stand a chance.
BEVERLY. We're not playing for money.
BREEN. (*Laughs.*) Alright.
BEVERLY. Red or black?
BREEN. Red.

(THEY set up the checkerboard in silence.)

BEVERLY. I'll let you move first.

(THEY play.)

BREEN. So how long you been divorced?
BEVERLY. I didn't say I was ... (*SHE jumps one of his men.*) Less than a year. (*HE moves. SHE moves.*) He walked out one afternoon when I was in town. Didn't even tell me he was going.
BREEN. That's too bad.
BEVERLY. Isn't it. Why did you leave your wife?
BREEN. Wasn't working anymore.
BEVERLY. Did you tell her you were leaving?
BREEN. No. No, I never got to.
BEVERLY. I see. Just one day you weren't there. Crown me.
BREEN. (*Crowns her.*) I had my reasons.
BEVERLY. I'm sure.
BREEN. I think they were good reasons.
BEVERLY. I'm sure if my ex was out on a snowy Christmas Eve and found himself caught in a blizzard talking to someone like me, I'm sure he'd have good

reasons, too.

BREEN. Maybe.

BEVERLY. Probably.

BREEN. And Nola might be bitter like you.

BEVERLY. I'm not bitter. Crown me again.

BREEN. I told you you were too good for me.

BEVERLY. You're not concentrating.

BREEN. It's harder for me to talk about ... about my break-up than it is for you.

BEVERLY. Did you have any children?

BREEN. No. But three miscarriages.

BEVERLY. So that's why you—

BREEN. Crown me.

(SHE begins concentrating on the game.)

BREEN. You see, without going too deeply into the past, Nola had a substance abuse problem. She loved the white powder and when she didn't have it, she tended toward abuse. And there was the savings and the valuables and a few not really valuable heirlooms, and she'd disappear and then in a week or two come back and go through rehabilitation and then go through it all again. This happened a number of times. The last time, we were living in Athens. Athens, Georgia ... and it was the fall, and she and the new man with the powder decided to be snowbirds and go south for the winter. I imagine they gave new meaning to the term "snowbird." And after forty days and forty nights, the phone began to ring, and I didn't pick it up. It rang on and on for the next few weeks. But you see, I had left her. And I'll take your king. Crown me again.

BEVERLY. You're good at this.
BREEN. Haven't played in years.
BEVERLY. I'm sorry.
BREEN. Don't be.
BEVERLY. You've won.
BREEN. You still have a chance.
BEVERLY. Not really. You know, Howard Lee's going to be closing down at midnight.
BREEN. He is.
BEVERLY. He only stays open to midnight 'cause of the holiday.
BREEN. Are there any motels around?
BEVERLY. Not for ten or twelve miles.
BREEN. I can make it.
BEVERLY. Don't be ridiculous. Howard Lee or I, neither one of us is going to let you go out in this storm.
BREEN. Well, I got to do something.
BEVERLY. If you'd like, you can stay at my place.
BREEN. That's nice of you to offer.
BEVERLY. You've got to have some place to stay, and Howard Lee's got a family.
BREEN. Beverly, with all the things that's happened the last few years ... I just don't have a hankering for a woman's body.
BEVERLY. What?
BREEN. I said I just don't—
BEVERLY. I heard what you said.
BREEN. One of the reasons I wear the ring.
BEVERLY. I think maybe you misunderstood the offer.
BREEN. Maybe so.
BEVERLY. I thought you were stranded here. That

your car had gone off the road and that you didn't have a place to stay. I thought you needed that. It didn't have anything to do with any hankering on my part.

BREEN. I'm sorry. I didn't mean—

BEVERLY. You damn well should be. You think I got a hankering?

BREEN. How should I know?

BEVERLY. Do I act like a woman who's got a hankering? Is that what you thought?

BREEN. I couldn't tell.

BEVERLY. Well, I'll tell you. I don't.

BREEN. What do you expect me to think?

BEVERLY. Certainly not what you thought!

BREEN. We just met. We haven't known each other for thirty minutes and you're asking me to spend the night.

BEVERLY. It's a big house. There are three bedrooms.

BREEN. How was I to know that— Or—

BEVERLY. I told you it was two and a half stories.

BREEN. Look, I'm sorry. I just think it's better to be up front.

BEVERLY. Doesn't mean you have to think the worst.

BREEN. There's nothing wrong with two people meeting and deciding to spend the night together. I just don't want to be with someone that way.

BEVERLY. You have made your point. And neither do I. So forget I offered. And shut up about it. Alright?

BREEN. Alright!

(There is a long silence. BEV stomps around a bit, getting herself coffee or something. BREEN does not move.)

BEVERLY. If you want any more coffee, get it

yourself.
BREEN. I will.

(Again, there is a long silence. Then—)

BREEN. (*Singing.*) Oh, holy night/The stars are brightly shining/It is the night of the dear Saviour's birth.

(BEVERLY starts laughing.)

BREEN. (*Looking at her, smiling.*) Long lay the world in sin and error pining/Til he appeared and the soul felt its worth.

(SHE smiles and and begins singing.)

BREEN amd BEVERLY. A thrill of hope/The weary world rejoices/For yonder breaks a new and glorious morn/(*SHE is really into it.*) Fall on your knees/Oh, hear the angel voices/Oh, night divine/Oh night (*To end of chorus.*)
BEVERLY. I missed them this year. They always drive around from house to house on Christmas Eve and carol. Didn't make it out because of the storm.
BREEN. I'm sorry if I made you—I didn't mean ...
BEVERLY. I know. I was being romantic. It's a problem I have. Romantic.
BREEN. Oh.
BEVERLY. Not that kind of romantic. Romantic in a—It's just that I'm very lonely ... I don't have anyone ... you don't have anyone ... and to try and cure your loneliness, you go back to happier times ... and ... well, in

THE ROAD TO NINEVEH

a way, we're a couple of orphans in a snowstorm on Christmas Eve ... and I felt like there's a reason for that. Maybe this happened so we'd not be alone. Silly romantic fantasies ... when I was younger, before I married ... they got me into all kinds of problems.

BREEN. I can see how they would.

BEVERLY. Un-hun.

BREEN. Do you allow a man to change his mind?

BEVERLY. It depends.

BREEN. I'd like to reconsider your offer if I may.

BEVERLY. You may.

BREEN. Thanks.

BEVERLY. Spoonbill ...

BREEN. Uh?

BEVERLY. I don't want you to be spooked, so I need to tell you I went a little crazy.

BREEN. Yeah.

BEVERLY. I just sort of let go ... and I went out and bought presents and wrapped one up for a man without putting his name on it, and I got one for myself ... and I can't for the life of me remember what it is ... and there's a big old Christmas tree with strung popcorn ... and food ... there's a house full of food and logs brought in for the fireplace.

BREEN. It sounds like you had this all planned.

BEVERLY. I didn't. I swear I didn't. I just went crazy.

BREEN. I don't have any present for you—

BEVERLY. There's one under the tree.

BREEN. I guess Santa must have brung it.

BEVERLY. Must have. Why don't we go. I like to open my presents on Christmas Eve.

BREEN. Howard Lee wanted us—

BEVERLY. We'll leave him a note. I got a present for him and Mary Ann. (*Takes it out.*) Matching key chains with Donald and Daisy Duck. That's their C.B. handles. (*Writing note.*) We went to open our Christmas presents. See you the day after Christmas. Beverly—You want to sign your name?

BREEN. Might as well. (*HE does.*)

BEVERLY. Spoonbill, I hope you like green beans.

BREEN. I'm not crazy about them. But they're edible.

BEVERLY. You're having them. So you might as well enjoy them.

BREEN. You are very weird.

BEVERLY. Me? You're not so normal yourself.

BREEN. Did you make snow ice cream when you were a kid?

BEVERLY. Of course.

BREEN. Why don't we do that? Why don't we gather a bunch of snow and make some ice cream?

BEVERLY. And maybe tomorrow we can build a snowman. What do you think?

BREEN. We'll see.

BLACKOUT

THE END

COSTUMES AND PROPS

Costumes are simple and contemporary; no attempt should be made to make them seem "rustic."

Props: Christmas decorations, Christmas tree, checkerboard, checkers, coffee cups, coffee maker, sugar, cream, cream pitcher, soup, wrapped present.

32 OFF-OFF BROADWAY FESTIVAL PLAYS

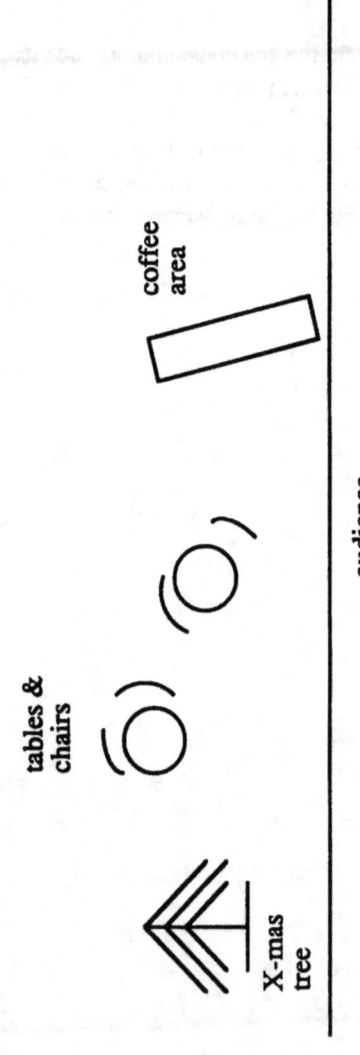

The Road to Nineveh

CORRECT ADDRESS
by
Judd Lear Silverman

Correct Address was developed in readings in Charles Maryan's Playwrights/Directors Workshop under the direction of the author. Jeff was first played by Kelly Masterson and then by Jeff Oppenheim. Terrence Keene was Adam.

An early version of *Correct Address* was presented by Love Creek Productions in their Spring 1991 Mini One-Act Festival. Adam was played by Kevin Reifel and Jeff was played by Gordon Wilk. The director was Christine Linkie.

Correct Address was presented by Theater Factory in June 1992 at The Nat Horne Theater. The director was Frank Trezza.

ADAM..Michael Johnston
JEFF ....Tony Dougherty

A subsequent production was presented in August 1992 by the Hudson Theater Artist Guild. The director was Richard Sabellico. Jonathan Arak was the Assistant Director.

ADAM...Brian Shait
JEFF ....Robert Sella

CHARACTERS

ADAM, late 20s — early 30s

JEFF, late 20s — early 30s

The time is the present.

AT RISE: ADAM is packing a large, heavy duty cardboard box. Surrounding him are a few remaining stacks of books, a few records, some large manilla envelopes, a few pieces of bric-a-brac (some already wrapped in newspaper, some not) and a five by seven index card. Also on the floor are some old newspapers for packing, mailing tape, twine, scissors, a big black magic marker—and all the other familiar packing and mailing tools. ADAM appears to be talking to someone offstage.

ADAM. Thank God. Just a few more items and we're *finally* done. Pack it up, ship it off to Cleveland.

JEFF. (*From offstage.*) To the ancestral burial grounds.

ADAM. Breakables carefully wrapped in at least three sheets of newspaper apiece. Files and documents carefully marked and placed in individual envelopes. (*HE picks up the index card and checks out the address.*) Correct address and zip code, including the four digit secondary code for a total of nine digits, lest there be any mistake.

JEFF. (*Offstage.*) You're anal.

ADAM. Thorough. That's thorough. I don't want to take any chances that it won't reach its proper destiny.

JEFF. (*Enters.*) You mean destination.

ADAM. Arriving at your proper destination is your destiny, isn't it?

JEFF. No. Arriving at any destination is destiny, regardless of how proper it is.

ADAM. True.

JEFF. In fact, I suspect most of life is about not ending up in the place we planned or intended to.

ADAM. Well, this isn't where I expected we'd end up. Certainly not where I expected you'd end up. (*Pause.*) Not where I expected I ...

JEFF. *(A Southern accent.)* Things have a way of turning out so badly. (*JEFF picks up from among the bric-a-brac a little ceramic elephant planter.*) Jeez, I'd forgotten about this little bargain.

ADAM. Flea market find. I'll let you have it for three dollars.

JEFF. Two!

ADAM. It's an antique!

JEFF. Two! I only paid two dollars for it.

ADAM. And the mother gets it for two dollars!

JEFF. You'll notice that the trunk is raised in the air. The lady who sold it to me said that's a sign of good luck.

ADAM. (*Shoots Jeff a look.*) In that case, you should get your money back.

JEFF. Thanks a lot. How come you're not keeping it?

ADAM. Who wants a defective good luck charm? Besides, this apartment already looks like tsatske heaven.

(*JEFF hands the elephant back to ADAM, who wraps it in newspaper and puts it carefully in the box. A pause.*)

ADAM. I'm keeping the scripts.

JEFF. Dear Mother wouldn't know what to do with them anyway.

ADAM. Enshrine them.

JEFF. Embalm them.

ADAM. Some of them should have been embalmed!

JEFF. Hey, now you're being critical!

ADAM. I thought my duty to be supportive had ended.

JEFF. Now you're supposed to deify me.

ADAM. Once I pack and seal this box, it's over.

JEFF. You won't get off that easy. (*Pause.*) Anyway, they're safer with you. You'll know what to do with them.

ADAM. How will I know?

JEFF. You'll know.

ADAM. All right, but don't blame me if you're not satisfied—

JEFF. I won't. (*Pause.*) Clothing?

ADAM. Mother didn't want any of it.

JEFF. Not even the sweater she made me? The one you are so proudly modelling for us today?

ADAM. I didn't mention it to her. I'm keeping it for myself.

JEFF. Greedy.

ADAM. You betcha. I deserve it.

JEFF. Scripts and sweaters.

ADAM. Hey, I'm making out on this deal like gangbusters!

JEFF. Not to mention paintings, drawing, etchings.

ADAM. Which we bought together.

JEFF. You might have offered.

ADAM. Screw you! (*Pause.*) Should I have?

JEFF. Oh, I really don't care, I was just kidding.

ADAM. No, seriously, should I have? I mean she is your mother.

JEFF. Sweetheart, you don't owe her anything just because she's my mother.

ADAM. But that's just it. She *is* your mother.

JEFF. For thirty-three years running ...

ADAM. Not anymore.

JEFF. Cut out the hearts and flowers. No time. Got to get that package off to the post office.

ADAM. Forever your errand boy. (*Pause.*) Seriously, I'm wondering if I—

JEFF. No! You've handled things splendidly. You have just as much right to keep things as she does. Possession is nine-tenths of the law. Possession is the better part of valor.

ADAM. That's discretion.

JEFF. I never noticed how many proverbs are preoccupied with fractions.

ADAM. Yes, you have. There is no cliché that you haven't exploded, no homily you haven't ransacked, no turn unstoned, nothing in the english language that you haven't investigated with the fervor of Woodward and Bernstein.

JEFF. Showing your age, dear.

ADAM. Fuck you. (*Pause.*) Words have never been your stranger.

JEFF. I write the words that make the whole world speak—

ADAM. I could send Mother your Barry Manilow records.

JEFF. Record. I only have one.

ADAM. Two.

JEFF. One!

ADAM. (*Holding the records up.*) I found another one when I was cleaning.

JEFF. It's a vagrant. It wandered in. Maybe the other record was pregnant when I bought it.

ADAM. Two for the price of one, then. Boy, what a

good deal!

JEFF. Hey, in your present financial condition, you shouldn't scoff at bargains. Anyway, you can keep them.

ADAM. Thanks, but those I think Mother can have. (*Pause*.) Anyway, I never knew you were such a Manilow fan.

JEFF. A man of many secrets.

ADAM. I'll say.

JEFF. Secretive secretions. (*JEFF picks up from the floor a smallish porcelain picture frame from the floor.*) You were gonna send her this?

ADAM. Sans picture, of course.

(*ADAM takes it from him, removes the picture from the frame. HE looks at it a moment, looks at Jeff. JEFF retrieves the picture from him and studys it. ADAM begins to wrap the little frame in newspaper.*)

JEFF. My God, look at us. We were babies.

ADAM. Four years ago. We were hardly babies.

JEFF. Well *I* was! We were new to each other at least. (*Pause*.) Hi there, handsome.

ADAM. Hi yourself.

JEFF. Jeff Parkway.

ADAM. What a name!

JEFF. Hey, it's mine! We lived by one, I claimed it. And you are?

(*ADAM looks at him a moment, not really wanting to play along, but JEFF fixes him with "that" look. What can he do?*)

ADAM. Adam Dunn.

JEFF. Thy will be.

ADAM. A joke that has never improved with time. What do you do for a living?

JEFF. I'm a playwright.

ADAM. So, what do you do for a living?!

JEFF. Free lance office work. You?

ADAM. Graphic design. Free lance at the moment.

JEFF. Your lance is free at the moment?

ADAM. You never said that.

JEFF. I should have. So are you working now?

ADAM. (*Exasperated.*) Actually, yes! I am trying to finish packing this box! Otherwise—

JEFF. Otherwise what?

ADAM. Cleveland will be on the phone again.

JEFF. Stop worrying about her!

ADAM. Easy for you to say. (*Pause.*) I'm sorry I don't like your mother.

JEFF. Then eat your vegetables. Sorry, old cannibal joke.

ADAM. I should be closer to the woman who raised you.

JEFF. You love corn on the cob, too, but you don't want to be closer to the farmer who raised that!

ADAM. How do you know?! (*Pause.*) I just know it wasn't easy for her.

JEFF. Excuse me?!

ADAM. I mean, alone and all.

JEFF. Short of the monthly check, she didn't miss Daddy Dearest at all and neither did I.

ADAM. You didn't know him.

JEFF. I didn't miss him.

ADAM. Bullshit. You missed not knowing him.

JEFF. Now you're starting to sound like her.

ADAM. Don't get us confused, dear. We're two distinctly different people.

JEFF. So is that *your* theory? That I'm in need of a father figure? Is that why I chose you?

ADAM. I'm not your father, your mother, or even your great Aunt Bertha.

JEFF. So what are you?

ADAM. I am ... tired. I am ... broke. I am ... going to finish packing so I can take this to the post office before it closes and get on with my life.

(During the next section, ADAM puts the last few items in carefully on the top and begins to wad up newspaper to put in for added protection.)

JEFF. Brilliant, Watson!

ADAM. Thank you, Holmes. Except, why am I always Watson and you Holmes?

JEFF. Elementary, my dear Watson. I am Batman, you are Robin.

ADAM. They killed Robin off.

JEFF. I am the Green Hornet, you are Cato.

ADAM. Who made me the perpetual sidekick? Couldn't we have taken turns?

JEFF. No! Because you were always the partner who had to be saved. You were always waiting to be saved.

ADAM. And you couldn't let yourself be helped.

(Pause.)

JEFF. (*Wryly.*) The perfect blend.

ADAM. Like coffee.

JEFF. More jolt than coffee.

ADAM. More flavor than instant.

JEFF. Able to jump tall buildings in a single bound! Look, up in the sky, is it a bird? Is it a plane?

ADAM. Is it a birdbrain?

JEFF. Yes! It's super-birdbrain! By day, secretly disguised as mild-mannered playwright, Jeff Parkway—

ADAM. You were never mild-mannered a day in your life.

JEFF. Well, mannered, then. You have to admit that I was mannered.

ADAM. Manic.

JEFF. Maniac.

ADAM. Bingo! My friends would ask, "Who was that serial killer I saw you with last night?" "That was no serial killer, that was my lover."

JEFF. (*A burlesque drum.*) Buh-dum-bum.

ADAM. Thank you, thank you. For my next trick —I shall actually remove this heavy, mother-fuckin' box from this overcrowded apartment and ship it where the sun don't shine.

JEFF. Don't be absurd. Cleveland is absolutely tropical this time of year. And what's this about my mother having illicit relations with a packing container?

ADAM. It'd be the most fun she's had in years.

JEFF. Whooo, you really don't like her, do you?

ADAM. Let's not talk about her.

JEFF. Why not? Why hold back? It's just the two of us.

ADAM. No, I just—I just won't talk about her, that's all.

JEFF. Well, *she's* not dead yet, so it's not improper to speak ill of her.

ADAM. Jeff—

JEFF. What?

ADAM. Nothing. (*ADAM has now finished packing the box and has begun to fold the top panels. HE takes some brown cellophane mailing tape stretches it over the top in several layers, using the scissors to cut the tape.*) I hate this tape.

JEFF. So why use it?

ADAM. Because there are certain ways to mail a package. This is the tape they now want at the post office and so *that is what I'm going to use*!

(*Pause.*)

JEFF. Say, while you're there, maybe you should take the civil service exam. They *need* good men like you. And you could certainly use—

ADAM. (*Quietly.*) Shut up. (*Pause.*) I wonder how much I should insure this stuff for? The man at the post office always acts like you should have brought in an appraiser.

JEFF. What's it worth to you? Probably more than it's worth to her.

ADAM. Will you cut it! If she wants this ... junk, she can have it.

JEFF. She'll probably throw half of it out. Or burn it and save the ashes.

ADAM. That does seem to be her style.

JEFF. I always thought it would have been far more interesting if she'd had my grandmother mounted and

stuffed.
    ADAM. I'd like to see her mounted and stuffed.
    JEFF. And me?
    ADAM. Stuffed.
    JEFF. Poor boy.

(THEY look at each other a moment. ADAM looks away, finds the index card and starts to address the box with black magic marker.)

    ADAM. Well, I got to get this—
    JEFF. (*Finishing the sentence.*) ... to the post office, I know. God knows, you don't want to miss the last pick-up.
    ADAM. You were my last pick-up.
    JEFF. Very good. The years with me have taught you lots.
    ADAM. I'm a fast study.
    JEFF. In some areas. Yeah, I don't know where Mother's obsession with saving ashes comes from. Maybe she was a chimney sweep in a previous life.
    ADAM. Your mother never had a previous life.
    JEFF. That would explain her arrested state of development.
    ADAM. Your mother—

(Pause.)

    JEFF. What?
    ADAM. Nothing.
    JEFF. Go on!
    ADAM. What's the point? It's all over anyway.

JEFF. Is it? Obviously not.

ADAM. No?

JEFF. No! Otherwise ... you wouldn't be agonizing over that God-damned box like you were shipping out The Pietà! (*Pause.*) Doesn't The Pietà have a broken nose or something?

ADAM. What?!

JEFF. The Pietà? Michelangelo's Pietà! Doesn't the madonna have a broken nose?

ADAM. You mean like Streisand or something?

JEFF. No, remember some madman in the 70's got into the Louvre or wherever they keep it and smashed her nose? Fingers, too, I think. Claimed he was Jesus and said that wasn't how it was.

ADAM. What on earth made you think of that?

JEFF. Mother love. If Jesus has come back and smashed his mom's schnozz—

ADAM. Jesus is not back. He never left, according to some.

JEFF. Maybe he's sharing an apartment with Elvis.

ADAM. You're sick.

JEFF. Yes, well ... That would be fun. Send my mom a picture with me, Jesus and Elvis, arms around each other's shoulders, posed in front of the fireplace.

ADAM. She probably wouldn't be able to distinguish between the three of you.

JEFF. It would make one of those great greeting cards!

ADAM. Limited edition, I'm afraid.

JEFF. Everything, kid, is a limited edition. Everything has limits.

(Pause.)

ADAM. Yeah, and speaking of limits, if I don't get this to the post office, it'll be too late.

JEFF. There's always tomorrow.

ADAM. And tomorrow and tomorrow and tomorrow. I've held onto this for far too long. If there's one thing I don't want, it's another phone call from your mother.

JEFF. Let it ring off the hook. Let the machine answer it. "Hello, I'm not in and if it's Jeffrey's mother, the package is lost in the mail somewhere. Beep."

ADAM. I want it out of here.

JEFF. Do you?

ADAM. Yes!

JEFF. You sure?

ADAM. Yes.

JEFF. Then you can get on with it.

ADAM. Right.

JEFF. Nice, tidy, neat new life.

ADAM. (*Quietly.*) Yeah.

JEFF. That's really all you need to do, right? Get rid of the box?

(ADAM looks away.)

JEFF. It's gonna be all right. You're just ... (*Pause.*) Hey, they even fixed The Pietà's nose and hands. If they can do that—

ADAM. If they can put a man on the moon—

JEFF and ADAM. (*Together.*) —why can't they cure the common cold?

ADAM. I really have to—

JEFF. —go to the post office, I know, I know. You

know, you're getting repetitive in your old age.
  ADAM. At least I'm gonna make it to my old age.
  JEFF. Are you so sure of that?

(Pause.)

  ADAM. Yes. Yes, I am.
  JEFF. Good, good. That's the spirit.
  ADAM. Coming from you, that doesn't mean much.
  JEFF. Thanks a lot. Don't you think I—
  ADAM. Look, let's not—
  JEFF. Let's not what? If you can't say what you're thinking, what you're feeling *now*, then why bother trying to live to one hundred?
  ADAM. I've got to—
  JEFF. You're not leaving this goddammed apartment until you say it!

(Pause.)

  ADAM. What do you want me to say? That I miss you? That I'm lonely? That I'm scared? Is that what you want me to say? I don't have a hard time admitting any of that! I admit that everyday, that's no news. I admit it.
  JEFF. You mean that's permissible for the grieving widow. Responsible feelings. Suffering as an art form.
  ADAM. Screw you.
  JEFF. Why can't you admit what you really feel?
  ADAM. To who? To you?
  JEFF. Isn't that what you wanted to do all along? Isn't that why you're so angry?!
  ADAM. I am not angry!

JEFF. Bullshit! You're seething!

ADAM. I am *not* gonna do this!

JEFF. Why don't you say it? Why don't you get it off your fucking chest once and for all? I mean you wanted to, you know you wanted to, you were saving it up, storing it all up for that one moment to explode—

ADAM. And I never got the fucking chance! I never got the fucking chance to even say good-bye! You son of a bitch!

JEFF. I'm sorry, baby—

ADAM. Maybe if you had said something, if you had had some guts—

JEFF. It wasn't so easy.

ADAM. How could you have gone all those years and never told her? How could you never have told your own mother who you were, until the very end, until it was too late—

JEFF. She was my mother, I couldn't—

ADAM. You fuckin' coward! You denied everything! You denied *me*!

JEFF. I never denied you. Everyone in the world knew about us. I presented you to the whole world as my love.

ADAM. Except to your own mother!

JEFF. Adam, she would never have understood!

ADAM. You got that right! She sure didn't! And when you got sick and you still didn't tell her and she wanted to know what was wrong, then, even then you couldn't tell her!

JEFF. Adam, I—

ADAM. So she tells you to fly home to Cleveland like a good little boy so she can take care of you, help you get over your "flu." No need for your "roommate," that nice

Adam to fly with you, why should he be burdened! And when you ended up in the hospital, with a doctor telling her what you knew long before you got there, who does your loving mother blame? Me! That's who! Me! She thinks I killed you! She thinks I turned you into this ... *freak show* that took her little boy away and *she blamed me!* She wouldn't let me speak to you! She didn't even tell me you were in the hospital until it was all over! She told me I was pestilence! She told me I was diseased! And she wouldn't even let me come to your fucking funeral, man, she wouldn't let me come to your fucking funeral!

(Pause.)

    JEFF. I'm sorry, baby, I'm so sorry.
    ADAM. She wouldn't ...
    JEFF. I should have told her, I should have prepared her better, I know, it's my fault
    ADAM. I didn't even get to say good-bye.
    JEFF. Oh, Adam, I love you!
    ADAM. Fuck that! Fuck that! The bitch couldn't understand that I lost you, too! Not just her, *me!* Me too! I hurt! I lost you! But all she could hear was her own need. I want my son's things! Send me his things! His things!
    JEFF. I know.
    ADAM. Why? Why?!

(Pause.)

    JEFF. Because she was my mother. Because every man in her life wasn't who she thought he was—my grandfather, her husband ... me. And as much as I couldn't deal with her, she was my mother and I did love her and I couldn't ... disappoint her.

ADAM. But you did anyhow.

JEFF. I know. And I have to live with that.

ADAM. No, you had to die with that! And you disappointed me, too! You fucking disappointed me, too!

JEFF. I know.

ADAM. You fucked up, Jeffy! You made a mess of everything! Your mother is destroyed and so the fuck am I!

JEFF. No! *You're* not destroyed unless you choose to be. My mother never could understand and maybe she never will. But you have a choice because you *can* understand it! You don't have to be destroyed. You understand.

ADAM. But I love you!

JEFF. And you know I love you. And you'll always know that.

(Pause.)

ADAM. I want you out of my life. I want you out of my head. I want you out.

JEFF. And so now you gotta get to the goddamned post office with that package and then I'll be gone, right?

ADAM. I want you out of here. Now.

JEFF. You think that by shipping that box off to my mother that you'll be rid of me, that I'll be out of your life forever, and it's not true. I'm not just items to be packed in a cardboard box or a sweater or a Barry Manilow record. You don't get rid of me that easily. I'll always be in your head somewhere.

CORRECT ADDRESS

ADAM. I want you out. Now.

JEFF. Were you afraid you'd forget me? Is that why you waited three months to send the goddamned box?! Why the procrastination? Did you really think you needed to hold onto me that way? Adam, it doesn't take a fucking box to keep me with you. I'll always be with you. (*Pause.*) But Adam, I refuse to be your jailer. You have to get on with things. I want you to.

ADAM. Why should I care what you want?

JEFF. You gonna spite me by being a martyr? You think that's gonna hurt me?! You haven't even gotten yourself a decent job in three months and I *know* how empty your savings account is! That's just stupid! Get on with it! Don't worry about remembering me! You won't forget. Just get on with it!

(*Pause.*)

ADAM. She said I was diseased. Maybe I am.

JEFF. Stop it. We played safe.

ADAM. So what happened?

JEFF. The past.

ADAM. The past. And the future?

JEFF. You tested negative when we met. If you're worried, test again.

ADAM. Why bother? So I can know if my time's on a taxi meter?

JEFF. So that you can get on with life. With other people. (*Pause.*) You really don't have to send that stuff to my mother, you know.

ADAM. It's all right. I want to.

JEFF. You sure?

ADAM. Yeah, I'm sure. She's been disappointed enough.

(Pause.)

JEFF. I'm sorry, Adam.

(Pause.)

ADAM. I really would have been there till the end for you.
JEFF. I know that. *(Pause.)* It's getting late. You still gonna go?

(ADAM shakes his head and sinks to the floor by the box.)

JEFF. You could still make it.

(Pause.)

ADAM. I'll go tomorrow.

(ADAM folds his arms on top of the box and rests his head on his arms. JEFF waits a moment, then walks around behind him, sits down behind him, puts his arms around him from behind and rests his head on Adam's back.)

JEFF. *(Whispering.)* Let me go.
ADAM. I will. Tomorrow.

(ADAM leans his head back on Jeff's shoulder. JEFF tightens his embrace. ADAM closes his eyes.)

FADE TO BLACK

COSTUME PLOT

ADAM

Casual jeans
White or off-white T-shirt
"Hand-knit" sweater (summer weight cardigan)
Sneakers

JEFF

Off-white to khaki slacks
Off-white T-shirt
Sneakers

PROPERTY PLOT

Large corrugated cardboard box (to be shipped)
2 Smaller boxes (to be used for storage)
Various file folders
Various 10x15 manila mailing envelopes
7-10 Bound manuscripts
1 Large mailing label
1 Magic marker
1 Large index card or yellow legal pad (for Adam's checklist)
1 Roll plastic mailing tape
1 Scissors
1 Ceramic elephant with trunk raised (either small statue or planter)
1 Elaborate picture frame (ceramic, wood or metal)
2 Barry Manilow albums
Other assorted record albums
Assorted bric-a-brac for packing
Numerous sheets of newspaper (for wrapping each item)
Coffee mug

58 OFF-OFF BROADWAY FESTIVAL PLAYS

CORRECT ADDRESS - FLOOR PLAN

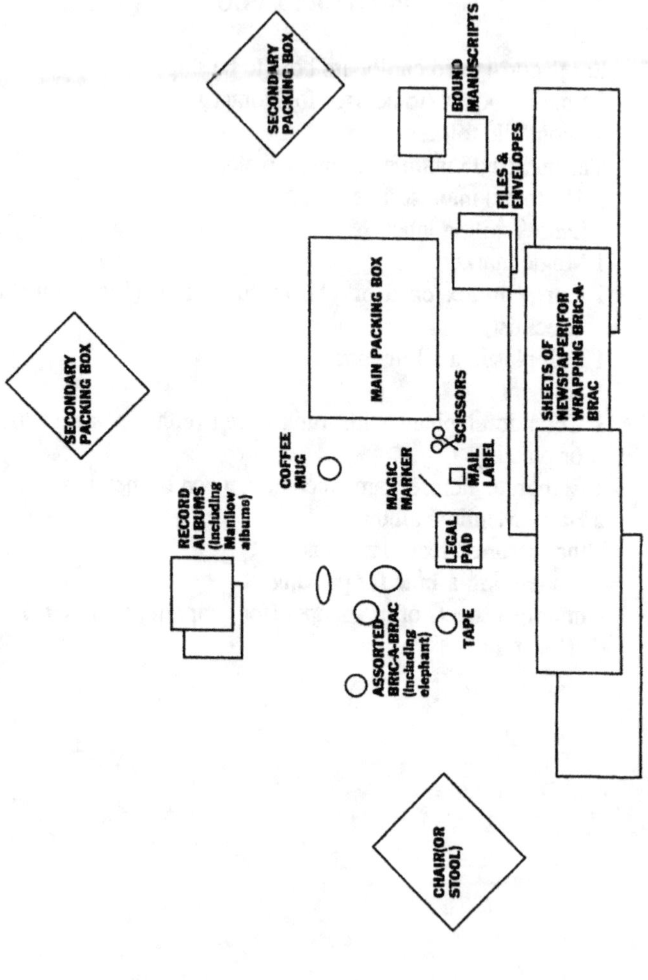

COWBOYS, INDIANS AND WAITRESSES

By Raymond King Shurtz

60   OFF-OFF BROADWAY FESTIVAL PLAYS

Cowboys, Indians and Waitresses was presented by Greenport productions. It was directed by Kurt Brungardt and had the following cast (in order of appearance):

PACKHARD REDHILLS ....John Vincent Vargas
YOUNG MAN ....Billy Asad
MANDY ....Linda Mannix
SHADOW LONG ....Kent Harding

Sets/Lights/Sound ....Jason Gordon

Cowboys, Indians and Waitresses was first produced at the Pioneer Folk and Theatre Festival, August, 1991 in Phoenix, Arizona. It was directed by Raymond King Shurtz and had the following cast (in order of appearance):

PACKHARD REDHILLS ....Jere Luisi
MANDY ....Elizabeth Scheffer
SHADOW LONG ....Raymond King Shurtz

CHARACTERS

SHADOW LONG: A cowboy, rugged, thirty-three.
PACKARD REDHILLS: A twenty-eight-year-old Navajo.
MANDY: A waitress, between twenty and thirty.

NOTE: There is an optional character, AN UN-NAMED MAN IN A SUIT, who sits at the table as the play begins. When the conflict arises between Shadow and Packard, he takes his newspaper and quickly goes in the bathroom. He emerges at the end of the play after Shadow and Packard finish their duel. He serves as a symbolic character, but is not imperative to the play.

TIME & PLACE

The present. Early morning.

The action takes place in its entirety in a small cafe adjacent to the Greyhound Bus Station in Flagstaff, Arizona. At the extreme stage right wall is a waitress station, indicated by a small counter where the waitress gets coffee and cups. The kitchen is in the back, unseen from stage. To the left of the waitress station, there is a counter facing the audience with three or four counter stools on its upstage side. At stage left, there is one small table with four chairs. The cafe atmosphere should have a disjointed western flavor; i.e. a couple of pictures indicating the romantic West; perhaps a rope hanging on the wall, etc.

NOTE: An optional setting would have these same

elements, except the romantic western atmosphere could be exaggerated by bright primary colors, tumbleweeds, barbed wire fence, and various "Hollywood" western symbols. In this particular setting the costuming would take on mythical western proportions, exploiting early Hollywood stereotypes.

BLACKOUT.
A sad, slow country and western ballad fades in.
LIGHTS slowly rise.
PACKARD REDHILLS is sitting on the far left stool at the counter. MANDY is pouring him a cup of coffee. PACKARD is obviously very hungover. As MANDY takes the coffee back to the wall, PACKARD removes a small bottle of whiskey from his pocket and pours a shot into his cup. MUSIC fades. Enter SHADOW LONG. HE carries a duffel bag and a rope. HE looks around the cafe and smiles broadly. HE's feeling good. HE walks over to Packard and smiles.

SHADOW. Hey Darlin'! I'll have me a black coffee when ya' get a minute ... And hey, fill up ma buddie's cup, on me by God and the good ole US of A.

(PACKARD ignores him.)

SHADOW. *(To Packard.)* How ya doin' pardner? Name's Shadow. Shadow Long, don't that beat all? My Daddy had one hell of a sense of humor.

PACKARD. How.

SHADOW. How? Did you say how? Sounds like you got one hell of a sense of humor yerself. Hey nurse! Get that coffee over here will ya?

MANDY. Hold your horses, cowboy, I'm comin'.

SHADOW. *(Sitting on stool.)* Them damn bus rides jest seem ta get longer and longer. *(Beat.)* Where ya headin' pard?'

PACKARD. Reservation.

SHADOW. Oh, yea? Which one? I'm purty familiar with just about every one out here in the west, 'course I don't know 'bout any a them eastern Indians, this is where the real fightin' took place, out here in the west.

PACKARD. (*Sardonically*.) Yea, big fight happen in west. Cowboy shoot Indian. Indian shoot cowboy ... one heap big fight ...

SHADOW. (*Laughing*.) You funnin' me, ain't ya chief? (*No response*.) I'm headin' ta Apache Junction, Arizona, got me a job wranglin' down there ... Ever been there?

PACKARD. Nope.

SHADOW. I ain't either. Seen sum pictures though ... S'got them Superstition Mountains smack dab in the middle of it. I'm sure you heard a that ... all those people disappearin' and the Great Spirit protectin' all that gold.

PACKARD. Great Spirit everywhere.

SHADOW. (*Mildly threatening*.) You wouldn't be makin' fun of me, would ya, chief?

PACKARD. Why would redskin want to make fun?

MANDY. I don't think he's in a talkative mood, cowboy ...

SHADOW. (*Chuckling*.) He's a strange one ... Hey, I used ta play with 'n Indian when I was a kid, he was ... Piute! You a Piute?

PACKARD. I'm a Navajo.

SHADOW. Oh, yea! Yer reservation's just north a here. Fact I jest passed through it. That is one purty sonoffabitch! (*SHADOW rises, and moves to the other side of Packard. Playfully*.) Hey! Since you are an Indian and I got you surrounded, so to speak ... why is it that every white man that sez he's got Indian in his blood, that Indian part always seems ta be Cherokee. Now why is that? I was thinkin' maybe ...

PACKARD. (*Directly looking at Shadow.*) I don't know.

SHADOW. You never thought about it?

PACKARD. No.

SHADOW. Yea ... well, that reservation north a here is damn colorful, I'll give it that. (*Beat.*) So ... whataya do up there ... raise sheep?

PACKARD. (*Rising.*) Make bow and arrow ... hunt Cherokee Indians!

SHADOW. Look, if ya don't like me why don't ya just say so 'stead a all this Indian bullshit. I was jest makin' time pass with a little conversation. Anythin' wrong with that?

MANDY. Cowboy, would you please jest calm down?

SHADOW. Calm down? This boy is actin' like I signed the reservation papers personally ... I wasn't even born. I don't feel sorry for anybody livin' in America!

PACKARD. I'm not looking for any sympathy, cowboy, I just want to drink my coffee, get on the bus and go home ...

SHADOW. I'll bet you gotta helluva lot more 'an I got chief! Every thing I own is right there in that bag.

PACKARD. Do you want me to give you a medal? (*Beat.*) I don't have anything to say to you ...

MANDY. Cowboy, please don't ...

SHADOW. If that's the way you want it, Chief. (*SHADOW turns his attention now to Mandy as SHE begins to clean up dishes on the table.*) What about you, honeypot? You got anything ta say ta ole Shadow?

MANDY. I'm sure I'll think of something.

SHADOW. Why don't ya come over here and let's me and you do a little communicatin'.

MANDY. (*Coming over.*) Alright, cowboy, what could you possibly say to me that you ain't said to probably a thousand other waitresses?

SHADOW. How 'bout you an' me just skippin' marriage an' jumpin' right ta the honeymoon?

MANDY. (*Nonchalantly.*) And just where is this honeymoon takin' place ...

SHADOW. (*Putting his hand to his heart.*) Right here, darlin'...

MANDY. Cowboy, you are just drippin' with sincerity. I believe that hand is just a little high for what you have in mind.

SHADOW. You don't give a man much of a chance do ya, darlin'.

MANDY. I'd say your chances are about one in a million the way you're goin' about it.

SHADOW. What could I do ta change those odds?

MANDY. Probably not much ...

SHADOW. Well maybe we oughta just back up to the basics of love.

MANDY. Your flirtin' technique could use a little overhaul.

SHADOW. I think we're capable of a little love conversation, I'm a man and you're a woman ... 'sides love is ... universal.

PACKARD. Miss, I'd like to pay for my coffee.

MANDY. Yessir. (*SHE writes out Packard's check.*)

SHADOW. Your bus ain't here yet, chief, what's your

hurry?

PACKARD. I guess the conversation is getting a little deep in here, Tex.

SHADOW. Well, we could talk about the weather if love's a little to much fer ya.

PACKARD. Love isn't something in my vocabulary, and if it was, it would be a cold day in hell when I discussed it with you.

SHADOW. What did I do ta you besides try ta be friendly?

PACKARD. You got up this morning ...

SHADOW. What did you say ta me?

PACKARD. You heard me ...

MANDY. If you boys wanna play with each other, you best take it outside.

SHADOW. (*Standing.*) Boyeeee! You got somethin' botherin' you ... way down deep inside ... I can feel it creepin' 'round this room. We got some serious goin's on here!

PACKARD. You got some nerve, mister!

SHADOW. You gotta snake inside you, chief, and it's jest eatin' your guts inside out.

PACKARD. You best just back off!

SHADOW. (*Excited.*) We got us trouble! Right here in River City! Goddamn trouble hangin' 'round your head like vultures 'round a road kill!

MANDY. (*To Shadow.*) What is the point of you doin' this?

SHADOW. The point is livin' life! Gettin' your senses all riled up! Havin' interaction with one another! Bein' alive, that's the point, darlin', bein' alive and knowin' it ...

(PACKARD moves over to the upstage chair by the table. MANDY takes the bill over to him. HE takes it, but doesn't move from his spot. SHADOW catches MANDY on the way back to the waitress station and starts to dance with her, possibly forcefully.)

SHADOW. Now, where was we, sweetheart?

MANDY. *(Pushing him away.)* We weren't anywhere ... You keep your hands off me!

SHADOW. I was jest gettin' ready ta tell ya how much I was in love with ya.

MANDY. You're just full of surprises ... did you want anything else with your coffee?

SHADOW. Just whatever the moment 'ull bring, sugar ... *(SHADOW turns to look at Packard.)* Thing's a little bit quieter over there fer ya,' chief?

PACKARD. You get your kicks out of antagonizing Indians?

SHADOW. I ain't here ta antagonize ya, Indian, I'm here ta rescue ya from the storms of life! *(Laughs.)*

PACKARD. *(Amazed.)* Are you for real?

SHADOW. *(Laughing.)* Well, I guess that depends on your point of view ... Some people say I'm too damn real fer ma own good ... I say, fuck 'em if they can't take a joke! *(Beat.)* Hey! Did you ever read that book ... uh, uh, *Bury My Heart at Wounded Knee*?

PACKARD. As a matter of fact I did read it ... That's my problem, slim,—disease and alcoholism on the reservation—I'm in mourning for all native Americans in the good ole US of A.

SHADOW. Do you know how many died in the Indian Wars?

PACKARD. I have a feelin' I'm just about to find out.

SHADOW. 'Bout a thousand. Do you know how many died in Vietnam?

PACKARD. No I don't ...

SHADOW. Well you don't know much do ya Indian ... fifty-six thousand died in that war ...

PACKARD. What is your point, cowboy ...

SHADOW. You got suicide in your eyes, chief. Don't take a genius ta figure that out. It could be soon or it could be later, either way you got a time bomb in ya jest tickin' away. Tick tock ... tick tock ... tick tock ... Yea, you got the eyes of a dead man ... you don't value your life, Indian ... If yer' gonna throw it away you should throw it away on somethin' that has meanin', 'stead of a bunch of Indian bullshit that don't amount to a hill o' beans ... Ya' got life in ya... ya oughta be damn glad ya got it! I knew some boys that wish they had what you got ...

(PACKARD picks up his bundle, preparing to leave. SHADOW moves closer to him.)

SHADOW. So, whataya do now? You gonna go back ta that reservation ta off yourself? How ya gonna do it? Put a bullet in your head? Drink yourself ta death?

PACKARD. *(Turns around to face Shadow. HE has a knife in his hand.)* I've had about enough of you, cowboy! I'm gonna scalp you right here in this cafe! That's what you want, isn't it?

(SHADOW moves around the table in a circular fashion. MANDY lets out a scream. SHADOW pulls a gun from under his jacket. HE points it at Packard's face.)

SHADOW. Comm'on, buddy! Life feels pretty fuckin' good right now, don't it?

PACKARD. (*Stares at Shadow. HE finally sits at the table and buries his head in his hands.*) Why are you doing this to me!

SHADOW. (*Holds gun to Packard's head.*) How does death feel to ya now? Pretty fuckin' cold, ain't it?

MANDY. Why don't you just let him be!

SHADOW. Let him be ta kill hisself and maybe someone else in the process?

MANDY. Process of what ...

PACKARD. If I want to slit my throat it's my goddamn right!

SHADOW. (*Puts his gun down on the table.*) The truth slips out ... Feels good ta get angry don't it ... Ya' get all that mad stuck down in your craw ... if ya don't let it out sometime it turns in ta a knife in there ... starts pokin' yer guts till ya fill up with blood ... if ya don't die of a belly full, ya start spittin' that blood all over the ground just as fast as ya can ...

(*PACKARD pulls out his bottle of whiskey and takes a long pull.*)

SHADOW. Trouble is, ya gotta find somebody ta clean up the mess ... (*Pause.*) Gawd, boy, you don't wanna off yourself, the whole damn Seventh Calvary may be waitin' fer ya ...

(*PACKARD looks up at Shadow in amazement. HE then starts to laugh uncontrollably. SHADOW starts to laugh with him. SHADOW takes Packard's whiskey and takes a long drink.)*

SHADOW. Look at us, goddamn cowboy and Indian, havin' a drink o' whiskey fer this son of a bitchin' ache we got inside a us. Let it rain!

MANDY. You're not supposed to drink in here ...

SHADOW. Would you rather have drinkin' or dyin'? How 'bout both? (*To Mandy.*) Would you get over here and show a little maternal instinct?

MANDY. (*Reluctantly walks over to Packard.*) Why would you want to kill yourself?

PACKARD. Why does anybody wanna kill themselves? Misery, I guess ...

SHADOW. Your problem, see, is ya ain't ever really connected with who ya are ... yer ancestry ... all the sorry sons-a-bitches before ya.

PACKARD. Whataya mean?

SHADOW. Well now, ya tol' me yer a Navajo Indian, right?

PACKARD. Yea.

SHADOW. Well that's a good start. Once ya get it through yer head that ya got this life stirrin' around in ya, ya start lookin' fer what it has ta do with ya, see ... I'm a cowboy, yer an Indian, she's a waitress ... Now, Indians got certain ways about livin' jest like cowboys do, and waitresses and so on ... Now, jest after I got back from 'Nam I went back ta rodeoin', but ma damn feet didn't work the same way. I got this gout thing while I was in the bush, fucked me up bad ... I could still sit a horse but I couldn't make any money ... so, I kicked around Montana and Utah gettin' ta feel a lot like yer feelin' now. One day

I was sittin' in a little cafe 'bout like this one, in Kanab, Utah, an' I had all o' this bullshit bottled up inside me ... I guess I felt guilty 'bout comin' home from the war with gout, when a hell of a lot a ma buddies didn't come home at all. I was sittin' there thinkin' maybe I ain't really a cowboy, maybe I'm jest a fucked up nobody with gout ... maybe I don't even know what a real cowboy is. Now, I had some pretty ripe ole Justin boots and a Stetson hat, and I knew I could ride a horse and rope a calf, but it didn't matter 'cause ma brain was all jumbly ... Well, I went down to a little gun shop in the middle a town there, and bought ole Jake ... prettiest little pistol you ever layed eyes on. Then I went and bought me five-fifths of Jack Daniels Sour Mash Whiskey, an' I heads out into the desert thinkin' about just endin' it all there. I drank some a that whiskey and started shootin' that gun. Fer five days I stayed out there ... shootin' that gun, drinkin' whiskey and yellin' at the moon. At the end of them five days, when the whiskey was down to a swaller' an' the bullits was runnin' low, I started ta think 'bout turnin' that pistol on ma self ... then it hit me ... Here I was! I'd been drinkin' whiskey and shootin' a six-gun for five days in worn out Justin boots, an' a worn out Stetson hat. Now I still didn't own ma own horse, but I knew I could ride them sons-a-bitches like nobody's business ... and friend, when I finally, durin' the course a all a this, stepped in that pile a cowshit ... I knew ... I was a cowboy, right outta the great American west. There was a tribe a cowboys before me, an' there'll be some after ...

PACKARD. I'm not sure what all that means ...

SHADOW. You don't know if you really are an Indian, do ya?

PACKARD. (*Chuckles.*) Look at me ...
SHADOW. Ain't got nothin' ta do with yer outsides ...

(PACKARD takes a swig of whiskey and lets out a long war cry. MANDY is startled. SHADOW laughs. PACKARD begins chanting and dancing around the cafe. HE gets down on his knees.)

PACKARD. Two wagon ... eight horsemen. Big fat woman with two children.

(SHADOW runs over to Packard with the whiskey bottle. HE lays down on the floor. HE motions Packard to lay down beside him. THEY take a drink of whiskey which now has begun to fuel their words.)

SHADOW. Lemme show ya somethin' I learned in the hospital. Now close yer eyes. Whataya see?
PACKARD. 'Bunch of squiggly lines.
SHADOW. Now use yer imagination ... Like this ... I see a little green valley in Montana full o' Appaloosa horses.
MANDY. You can't just do this here! I'm gonna get in trouble!
SHADOW. Lay down here, darlin', you're gonna see somethin'!

(MANDY reluctantly lays down.)

SHADOW. A little green valley filled with Appaloosa horses ... You try ...
PACKARD. There's a windmill down on the lower end

...

SHADOW. What do you see, darlin'?

MANDY. I see my job, floatin' out the window ...

SHADOW. The wind is blowin'...

PACKARD. I see ten sheep starin' up at the windmill, like it was God.

SHADOW. A hawk is soarin' in that wind ...

MANDY. I see my boss, walkin' in the door ...

PACKARD. I see grave markers, hundreds of grave markers, crosses and little stone circles ...

SHADOW. There's a lone cowboy on a black horse, smokin' a cigarette and watchin' the hawk ...

PACKARD. Spirits are rising out of the graves, singing of vengeance.

(MANDY rises from the floor.)

PACKARD. I see corn fields on fire ... children running. I see the great Kitoni, chief of my people long ago ...

SHADOW. The lone cowboy is thinkin' 'bout a Mexican woman ...

MANDY. Would you please get up before someone walks in here? You're not supposed to drink in here ... we don't have a liquor license ...

(SHADOW rises and grabs Mandy's arm. PACKARD lies on the ground. HE begins chanting again. SHADOW kisses Mandy on the mouth, and SHE pulls away, slapping him across the cheek.)

MANDY. You're crazy! You're both crazy! I'm

calling the police!

SHADOW. (*Pulls out his gun, cocks it and points it at Mandy.*) You don't want to do that, girl ... You're not gonna spoil what's goin' on here ... I'm gonna call it ... (*Proudly.*) The Day of the Dog.

MANDY. The day of the what? I wasn't even supposed to work today!

SHADOW. How come you gotta be so damn stubborn ... why don't ya just learn ta enjoy adventure! (*HE lowers his gun.*)

MANDY. This is not my idea of adventure. And don't you ever pull a gun on me!

SHADOW. I wasn't gonna shoot ya.

MANDY. I don't care! This is my territory! This is my reservation. And it may not be much but it's all I got ...

SHADOW. What do ya git outta workin' here?

MANDY. I get paid! I make a living! It might not be a great living but I can eat!

SHADOW. You ain't happy here ...

MANDY. I am very happy here!

SHADOW. You don't let yourself enjoy what the minute gives to ya, hell, I bet you don' even have dreams at night let alone the day! Yer lips taste like ole dried up lemons. An' I'll bet that's not the only place that's dried up!

MANDY. You are a cruel son of a bitch! You think you can just say and do any damn thing you want to 'cause you have a gun!

(*SHADOW gives Mandy his gun. MANDY points the gun at Shadow.*)

SHADOW. Now yer cookin.'

MANDY. (*Aggressively.*) Oh, I had dreams, alright, cowboy, but they got sapped up by a goddamned man ... you men sap up women's dreams like you sap up whiskey ... An' when you're done sappin' every ounce of juice she's got in her, you move on to the next sucker ... never looking back ... never seein' the carnage of what's left behind. You men talk about love and romance and all that bullshit, but when the honeymoon is over the only thing left is that shriveled up little worm between your legs, and where you can get a rise out of it again! Men go to war, cowboy, but women go to hell and back for you sons-of-bitches! Don't preach to me about dreams ...

SHADOW. Doesn't it feel good?

MANDY. Nothing feels good right now ...

SHADOW. Spit out the bad blood, darlin', I can take it ...

MANDY. Shut up! Shut your goddamn mouth you arrogant son-of-a-bitch! I hate men! Do you hear me? I hate 'em.

(SHADOW takes Mandy in his arms as SHE begins to cry.)

SHADOW. Doesn't it feel good ta discover the waitress in ya?

MANDY. Waitressin' is all I know ... It's the only thing I can do.

SHADOW. Believe me, it's enough ...

MANDY. Leave me alone!

PACKARD. (*Rises. HE takes a slug of whiskey.*) Me Packard Redhills!

SHADOW. What's that ya say, chief?

PACKARD. My name ... Packard Redhills! Named after Grandfather's Packard convertible and beautiful red hills of reservation! Packard grow up in Indian housing project. Packard eat many Kellogg's corn flakes ... grow up big and strong! Big Chief in Washington give Packard money for school ... Packard go on big bird to white man school in East, go to be medicine man. Poor Packard, he drink whiskey made by white brothers. He fail school, drink more firewater, spend all Big Chief's money ... Big Chief say, "Poor Packard, he not fit in with white brothers, poor stupid Packard." ... Packard go home to reservation to die in corn field ...

(Pause.)

SHADOW. You hate me, chief?
PACKARD. I hate what you represent to me.
SHADOW. Do you think you could kill a man?
PACKARD. Yes.
SHADOW. How does it feel ta be alive?
PACKARD. It feels ... better.
SHADOW. Would you like ta kill me?
MANDY. Would you quit pushing him! Stop it! Stop all this craziness!
SHADOW. I asked ya a question!

(PACKARD lets out another war cry in Shadow's face and then a series of war hoops.)

SHADOW. Alright, chief ... your gonna feel what it's like to really be alive. You're gonna experience what it's like ta have all your senses blown up like a goddamned stick a dynamite! Your adrenaline pumpin' like ten fuckin' locomotives! Hands that could squeeze rocks inta dust! Blood boilin' iron and steel just ta stay breathin', chief ... You wanna know, chief? You really wanna know what it's like? (*SHADOW goes to his duffel bag, and takes out a pigging string. HE lays it on the counter and takes a drink of whiskey.*) This is war, chief!

PACKARD. Aaaaaaaaaaaahhh!!!!

MANDY. (*To Packard.*) Stop it! Stop acting like some wild Indian right this minute! (*To Shadow.*) Do something!

(*PACKARD starts a war dance. HE takes a tube of Mandy's lipstick from the counter and begins to apply it to his face like war paint. SHADOW begins to sing, "Streets of Laredo." HE takes his gun and starts to pantomime gun fighting poses. HE rolls over on the floor, taking aim at Packard while continuing to sing.*)

MANDY. Hey! Wait a minute, let's talk this thing out! Look, I'll drink down some of this whiskey and we can talk. Please!

SHADOW. You jest don't get it, do ya, girl.

MANDY. Get what? You two blowin' each other's brains out?

SHADOW. There ain't any stoppin' it now.

MANDY. This isn't gonna solve anything!

SHADOW. You're gonna have to write everything that happens down, in case I don't live through it ... And if I do die, I want you ta tell the sheriff it was all fair and square, self-defense ...

(PACKARD has gone into a deep trance in the center of the stage.)

SHADOW. I don't have any relatives ta speak of ... Oh, I got an aunt in Bluerock, Montana ... now there's a little book in my bag with an' address in it ...

MANDY. Don't you think you're blowin' this thing a little bit out of proportion? I think ...

SHADOW. (*Harshly.*) Don't think for Chrissakes! Just do what I'm tellin' ya ta do!

MANDY. Don't you yell at me!

SHADOW. You jest don't understand war, do ya.

MANDY. War?

SHADOW. War is somethin' we have ta do ... Don't you see how it makes us feel alive? Cleans out the bad blood between tribes. It's the stuff heroes are made outta ... He'll feel a lot better about himself ... don't ya see? It's all very clear, darlin'. We gotta clean up all his hatred once and fer all ...

MANDY. I'm not sure I understand all of that ...

SHADOW. I'm not askin' ya ta understand, I'm askin' ya ta do your sacrificial duty as a waitress and a patriotic American!

MANDY. I don't have the stamina for all of this, I'm just a waitress, I just pour coffee and keep as friendly as I can. I got a little boy to think about at home, I can't get mixed up in murder ...

SHADOW. (*Harshly.*) This is not murder! This is war, and there is a difference! This killin' is perfectly justified, it's heroic and honorable!

MANDY. It's ... a ... it's silly!

SHADOW. I'm gonna pretend I didn't hear ya say that. (*SHADOW goes over to Packard. HE moves his hand in front of Packard's face.*) Hey Indian, how much more time do ya need?

(*PACKARD begins to laugh hysterically. SHADOW joins in his laughter. THEY both fall in front of the counter laughing.*)

SHADOW. What is it, chief?
PACKARD. It's all this Indian stuff I'm doing. I've never done it before ... it feels so, so ....
SHADOW. What?
PACKARD. Natural ...
SHADOW. See what I mean about bein' a' Indian? Maybe you are one after all ...
PACKARD. Maybe I am ...
SHADOW. And I'll tell ya what it means ... it means havin' someone ta go home ta ... (*Beat.*) ... when you're the only one at home ...

(*PACKARD looks at Shadow as if some profound statement has been made that HE doesn't quite get. PACKARD rises. HE walks over to the table. MANDY sits at the counter in a daze.*)

PACKARD. I don't know if I can go through with it.
SHADOW. Now you ain't gonna get cold feet on me now are ya?
PACKARD. I don't know if I can ...
SHADOW. Fer Chrissakes, it's jest a little war. You'll feel a lot better about yourself if ya think about the

implications ... think about your people ... your children, your children's children ...

PACKARD. Why are you itchin' for war, cowboy?

SHADOW. It's not just war I'm itchin' for, it's redemption, it's liberation ... universal love! Savin' a life sometimes means takin' a life or two ...

MANDY. Why don't I get us all three some cherry pie ... I just made it this morning!

SHADOW. (*With unbelief.*) We don't want any cherry pie! (*SHADOW looks at Packard.*) Now ... what we'll be doin' is tyin' our arms together like this ... (*SHADOW puts his arm up, HE grabs Packard's arm and puts it next to his.*) We'll tie our arms together with this piggin' string ... (*To Mandy.*) Girl, git over here and tie our arms together.

(*MANDY does as she's instructed.*)

SHADOW. We'll put the knife in this hand. (*THEY both hold the knife.*) Now, when I give the signal ta Miss Kitty here, she'll fire this pistol and the duel'll begin ...

MANDY. I can't fire a gun!

SHADOW. (*Harshly.*) Now this duel is gonna have to begin with the firin' of that pistol fer it to have its true meanin', now you jest git that through yer purty little head!

(*MANDY starts to cry.*)

SHADOW. Calm down, calm down, there ... your jest findin' out the true meanin' of bein' a waitress ... isn't that what ya want? Isn't that what we all want?

MANDY. I can't be anything else ... (*Still crying.*)

SHADOW. Honey, don't ya realize what's happenin' here? Yer life is on the brink of changin' right at this point in hist'ry! This is the goin' forth of universal love, the war ta end all wars ... the sheddin' of blood ... sacrificial blood ... the last battle of the cowboys and Indians .... Jesus, God! Divine providence! (*Beat.*) Now, get over there and fire that pistol!

MANDY. Can't I just say "go" real loud?

SHADOW. You are startin' ta really try my patience! Get over there!

(*SHADOW and PACKARD brace themselves down center stage, and stare intensely into each other's eyes. MANDY moves stage left and holds the gun over her head. PACKARD chants softly to himself. SHADOW gives Mandy the signal with a nod of his head. MANDY fires the pistol and falls over backwards. SHADOW and PACKARD begin their "war." SHADOW pushes the knife very close to Packard's face. PACKARD pushes the knife towards Shadow's face. MANDY is pointing the gun at both of them, while hyperventilating. Suddenly, the knife is thrown out of their hands with a downward movement and then a thrusting upwards. The knife lands in the upstage area. BOTH MEN begin to struggle towards the knife, and each time THEY struggle close to it, MANDY kicks it away again. The struggle continues until the THREE OF THEM are completely exhausted. THEY come to rest in front of the counter. MANDY holds the gun in an extended position toward Shadow. HE gives her a threatening look and then rests a moment. SHADOW very slowly unties the rope around their wrists. HE rises and walks towards Mandy, backing her up. Finally, with a swift motion HE snatches the gun from her hand, and then retrieves his hat and returns to the counter. HE drinks. PACKARD rises, retrieves his knife and puts it away. HE sits at the counter. SHADOW looks at MANDY, who is still breathing heavily.)*

SHADOW. Would you please get us a cup a coffee?

(MANDY quickly gets the coffee and pours two fresh cups.)

SHADOW. Well, chief, I guess we can get on with the business of livin.'
PACKARD. I heard Apache Junction's a pretty wild place ...
SHADOW. The hell ya say ...

(THE UN-NAMED MAN IN A SUIT if used as a character returns to his place at the table.)

PACKARD. There's a lot of Pima Indians there.
SHADOW. Ya know ... if I could find the right place I might jest consider settling down ...
PACKARD. *(Tips his head back.)* I think I got a nose bleed.

(MANDY gets him some tissue.)

SHADOW. Was you really named after the red hills of that reservation?

PACKARD. That's what they tell me.
SHADOW. Darlin', have ya got a menu over there?
MANDY. Here. (*MANDY hands him a menu.*)
PACKARD. There's my bus ... (*PACKARD gathers his belongings. HE walks over to Shadow.*) If you ever go through the reservation ... it would probably be better if you just went on through ... no hard feelings, I just ...
SHADOW. Ya' don't need ta explain ... get your ass out ta that bus ... an' chief, next time ya think about killin' yerself, think twice 'cause I might be waitin' fer ya over there ...

(PACKARD exits. SHADOW looks at Mandy.)

SHADOW. Well ... do I get the girl at the end or not?
MANDY. You're gonna have to impress me first ...

(Keith Whitley's song, "It Ain't Nothin' a Little Bit of Love Can't Cure" fades in as the LIGHTS fade out.)

THE END

OPTIONAL ENDING

(PACKARD exits. SHADOW looks at Mandy.)

SHADOW. Well ... do I get the girl at the end or not?
MANDY. You're gonna have to impress me first ...
SHADOW. (*Goes to the un-named man in the suit at the table.*) How ya doin' pardner ... name's Shadow ... Shadow Long.

(An upbeat country and western ballad fades in as the LIGHTS fade out.)

THE END

COSTUME PLOT

MANDY

Coffee shop style waitress uniform.
Apron.
Rubber soled shoes.

SHADOW

Wrangler jeans.
Faded western shirt.
Large bandana.
Stetson hat (preferably white).
Justin boots (roper style).
Large trophy belt buckle.
Leather tooled belt.

PACKARD

Faded levis.
Black T-shirt.
Red bandana.
Cowboy boots.
Leather belt.

PROPERTY PLOT

PRESET:

ONSTAGE
Waitress station SR.
Cafe counter SR.
Three stools upstage of cafe counter.
Table SL.
Four chairs around table.
On walls are various Western motifs.
Poster of Ronald Reagan as a cowboy (optional).

On Waitress Station:
Bunsen type burner with two partially filled coffee pots.
One tray.
White cotton dish towel and a wiping rag.
Three coffee mugs.

On Cafe Counter:
Cafe-style napkin holders with napkins.
Plastic red and yellow condiment bottles.
Menu holders with menus attached to counter.
Coffee shop sugar and syrup containers.
Salt and pepper shakers.
Half-filled coffee mug.

Under Cafe Counter:
Cherry pie (optional).
Silverware.
Bus tray for dirty dishes.
One tray.

Cotton dish towel and a wiping rag.

On Floor behind Counter by stool:
Packard's backpack with whiskey bottle.

On SL Table:
Checkered table cloth.
Condiments.
Napkin holder.
Dirty dishes.
Newspaper.

PERSONAL PROPS

MANDY'S PROPS:
Guest checks.
Pencil/pen.
Purse with lipstick.
Apron.
Name tag.

SHADOW'S PROPS:
Old duffel bag.
Nylon rope (lariat).
Pigging string.
Chewing tobacco.
Western style white pearl-handle pistol (preferably small caliber) with blanks.

PACKARD'S PROPS:
Backpack with: pint of Old Crow whiskey; clothing.
Hunting knife.

COWBOYS, INDIANS & WAITRESSES

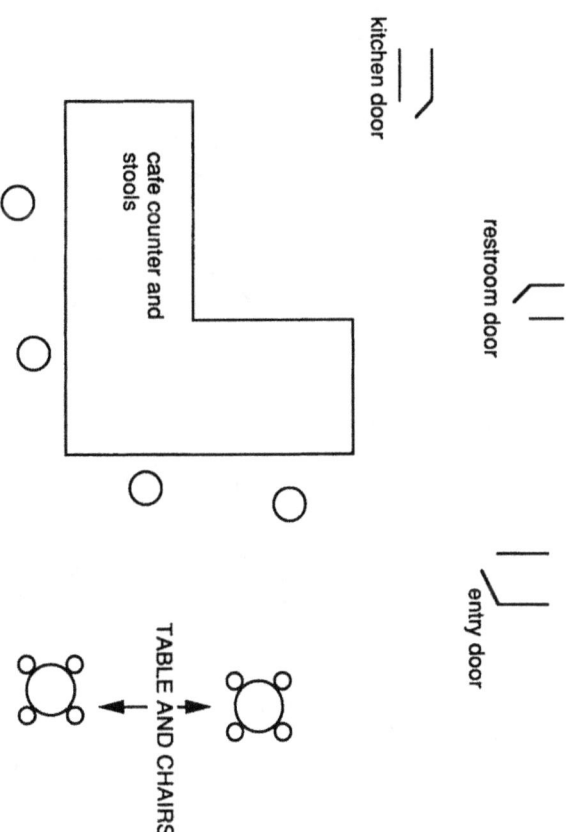

HOMEBOUND
by
Lyndall Callan

Homebound was first produced at the Westside Repertory Theatre, New York City on January 10th, 11th and 12th, 1992 starring Lyndall Callan. Stage management and artistic direction was by Michael J. Murnin.

HOMEBOUND

CHARACTERS

This is a one-woman show; however, here is the cast of characters who populate the main character's life. She is:

Lynnette Wilkes — age 17

Family members are:
Mama (Georgia) — age 34
Daddy (Frank) — age 40
Jake — age 16
Katie — age 14
Jimmy — age 11
Candy — age 7

Other characters are:
April Skinner — age 23 (her best friend and co-worker)
Bobby Jameson — age 19 (Lynnette's boyfriend)
Reverend Barre
Bernice Stetson (Bank teller)

A NOTE TO ACTORS AND DIRECTORS

With the exception of a table and two chairs, all of the scenery and props in this play can be created in space by the actor. Lighting can be used to delineate different settings, such as a church interior or bank. In the original production the actress wore jeans, sneakers, a t-shirt (and an apron in the kitchen and diner scenes). Minimal stage directions have been given to allow the actor and director to define the details of the action.

SCENE LOCATIONS

Scene 1: The Wilkes family kitchen
Scene 2: Daddy's bedroom
Scene 3: Kitchen (later that night)
Scene 4: The diner
Scene 5: Church interior
Scene 6: The bank
Scene 7: A car
Scene 8: North Rim Lodge—Grand Canyon, Arizona

TIME

A recent spring

PLACE

Goodnight, Texas

Scene 1

(LYNNETTE is wearing an apron. SHE is in the process of setting the kitchen table when the LIGHTS come up.)

LYNNETTE. I shouldn'ta done what to my hair, Mama? (*Looking up from her work, SHE sees her mother holding a family photo album.*)

Oh. What're you lookin' at those for? Uh-uh ... I hate pitchers. 'Cause everyone in 'em always looks so stupid ... Makin' creepy faces; wearin' funny clothes ... Well if you can't remember somethin' without a pitcher then you prob'ly didn't care too much about it in the first place.

No, I don't wanna see you an' Daddy's weddin' pitcher ... I'm not in it, am I?

No, I don't wanna see that pitcher of me lookin' like a prisoner. I do too know which one yer talkin' about—— 'Cause I was there; that's how I know. It's the one when I was seven an' I cut my own hair an' Daddy yelled at me an' Jake laughed when I got in trouble? See.

Oh, Mama. I cut it short 'cause I was tired of it, okay? Just what it sounds like—I was tired of it! If you'd've had your way I'd never've cut it an' it'd be hangin' all way down past my ass by now. I'd prob'ly be steppin' on it!

I did not cuss! What'd I say?

(Her brother Jake has just come in.)

Hey, Jake! J'a git the car workin'? (*Indicating their*

mother.)

She's all hopped up 'cause she thinks I cussed, but she won't tell me what it is I said.

I honestly don't know, Mama!

"Ass" is not a cuss word; it's in the Bible: "Jesus came ridin' into town on his ass."

I would too talk like this if Daddy wasn't sick; I'd jes' git hit for it is all.

No, Mama, I'm not sassin' you, I'm just tired.

'Cause I hate waitressin' ... Yes, I've noticed you work hard too, Mama, I was just sayin' ... I only meant ...

Please don't yell at me, Mama. (*Hurt.*) Okay. Never mind. Just forget it. *Forgit* it, Mama.

Want me to take Daddy's supper up to him? I *know* cut it up small—Give me a little credit, will ya? (*Picking up tray.*) Is he allowed to eat pork chops?

Jake, if he was restricted to a diet of lobster an' caviar, I think I'd know about it. In fact, if I ever saw a lobster in this house, *you'd* know about it, 'cause I'd scream my head off.

So what? I've seen pitchers of 'em. They're red, they've got about a million legs an' they're as big as a goat. I once seen a postcard from Atlantic City. (*SHE sticks her tongue out at Jake.*)

Okay, Mama, I'll bring it right up. (*SHE picks up the tray and carries it up to her father's room.*)

Scene 2

(*Daddy's bedroom.*)

LYNNETTE. (*Quietly.*) Daddy? You awake? I brought

you pork chops an' applesauce. Well, I'll just set it over here, an' if you want it, lemme know,'kay?

You feel pretty bad, huh? Well you don't jes' pass up pork chops an' applesauce for no good reason.

Want me to leave? 'Kay. (*SHE sits.*)

Want me to read to you? Don't have to read the Bible—I could read you somethin' else ... Last year in school we read a bunch of short stories an' there was one about this really dumb guy—Well, he wasn't exactly dumb, but he wasn't too bright, y'know? So these scientists did a experiment; it was with him an' this mouse. An' they gave this drug to the mouse an' the mouse got smarter an' smarter, an' they could tell, 'cause they made him run through these mazes an' he got better an' better at it. So they gave the drug to the dumb guy that they'd given to the mouse, an' the dumb guy started gittin' smarter an' smarter, an' he fell in love with this lady scientist. So he's real happy, right? 'cause he's smart an' he's in love, but after awhile he can see that it's only temp'rary, 'cause the mouse is gittin' slower an' slower an' weaker an' weaker ... an' ... um ... oh, shoot, I forgot the end.

Did'ja ever start tellin' a story an' you git halfway through it an' you forgit the end?

Daddy, do you think a seventeen year old girl could git senile? (*Laughing.*) I'm serious, Daddy! Sometimes at the restaurant, people order somethin' an' later on they say to me, "Hey now, you didn't forgit my pie now, did'ja?" an' I say, "Oh, no sir, I was just gittin' it!" when actually I'd forgot all about it.

Katie wants to go out tonight, an' she was gonna ask you if she could, but Mama said if she bothers you, she'd split her lip, so I told her if she *didn't* ask you, *I'd* split her lip. Anyway, she makes out like she's gonna be hangin' around with her friends, but I think she's got a boyfriend, 'cause when she stopped by the restaurant today after school there was a boy hangin' around the doorway waitin' for her. It coulda been Ned Miller's little brother, but I honestly can't tell. They're all growin' up so fast I don't even know what's what anymore. Katie tol' me that there's a boy in her class who shaves. Now, either he's been left back a few times or he's mighty mature for a fourteen year old!

Hey, Daddy, what's this? (*SHE holds out a cupped hand, fingers slightly spread.*) It's a dead one-a these! (*SHE flips her hand over.*)

You smiled, Daddy—Know what that means? "Order in the courtroom; the monkey wants to speak! No laughin', no talkin', no showin' of your teeth!"

When you git your voice back, I wanna hear you do that for the kids—Nobody does that as funny as you do, Daddy.

You *can* you know, but you've gotta want it. I don't believe in miracles, Daddy, but I believe if you want somethin' bad enough, you gotta try for it.

You an' me, we understand each other better 'n anyone else, 'cause I'm your first born, an' nothin'll ever change that. I'm the first person here or anywhere ever called you "Daddy."

Remember when I was seven, it was my birthday, an' I come home with a fat lip? Yeah, I'd kissed Dennis Taggart an' Faye Jameson punched me right in the mouth. I didn't know he was spoken for! An' after that, you taught me how to box. You were a real good teacher,

Daddy ... I blacked her eye.

Outa all five of us kids, I'm the one most like you. An' you didn't ever say, but I know you like me best.

An' you don't have'ta be able to talk for me to know what's goin' on with you. When you're havin' nightmares, it's like I can hear 'em ... I know when you're hurtin'—or scared. Yeah, the man who was stronger'n anyone else on earth—The man who rode me on one shoulder an' Jake on the other—The man who could yell louder, bowl more strikes, drink more beer ... I never thought I'd see that man scared.

Don't be, Daddy. You're gonna git better, I promise. If you die, I'll kill you.

I better go downstairs now an' help Mama feed the kids. I'll send 'em up after supper to kiss you goodnight.

(LIGHTS down slowly.)

Scene 3

(LIGHTS come up to half, revealing LYNNETTE asleep with her head on the kitchen table and her apron clutched in one hand. SHE starts suddenly as LIGHTS come up full.)

LYNNETTE. *(Gasping.)* Hunh?!? Ohmylord, Jake! You scared me! I was jes' restin' my eyes ... What time is it? Don't drink outta the carton.

(Stretching.) What're you doin' up at this hour? You gotta git up for school in the mornin'.

Yeah, but I can waitress while my brain's on vacation; you need to be able to pay attention in school. "Be alert; America needs more lerts." Ha ha ha. Oh no. I never called Bobby. Oh shoot. No, he's leavin' tomorrow for Fort Whatchamacallit or wherever the hell you go when you enlist. Tch. Shoot. (*Long exhale of resignation, eyes darting back and forth in thought.*)

Hmmm ... Well, if you do see him, give him a big kiss for me.

... *was* my boyfriend. Any jerk who goes in the army on purpose ... (*Shaking head.*) Nah, I'll be at work. I'm not acting stupid, I *am* stupid. I'm related to you, ain't I? (*Conspiratorially.*) Mama an' Daddy prob'ly didn't want you to know 'til you were older, but stupid is family trait they traced all the way back to our great, great, great Uncle Stupid. He was so stupid, one day he went out for cig'rettes, an' he forgot to come back. An' his stupid wife was left home all alone lookin' after forty-three stupid kids. An' pretty soon she forgot to feed 'em, an' they all died, 'cept one who was so stupid he ate the dog, so he survived an' he was our great, great Uncle Stupid. I'm not sure if it's Mama's side or Daddy's side.

DON'T DRINK FROM THE CARTON.

Y'know, if you're not gonna help out around here you may as well move out 'cause Mama's got enough to worry about without you settin' around actin' like a jerk.

Well, you could take on a little more responsibility. You could go fishin' with Jimmy or somethin'; start teachin' him stuff about bein' a man, y'know? Daddy taught you all that stuff—It'd be nice if you kinda—passed it along—y'know? Jimmy looks up to you. Or let him help you fix the car or somethin'. I don't know—

Somethin'. Okay? Jes'—try.

Hey, do you have any money? Saved up ... like a piggy bank or somethin'?

Oh. Nothin'. Never mind.

Remember when we were kids we got ten cents a week allowance? *That* was stupid. I guess it was supposed to teach us the value of money. But we used to go over to that wishin' well by the health center and pick up a little extra change when no one was lookin'. An' then we'd ride our bikes over to the candy store an' ruin our appetite for dinner. Not to mention our teeth. Well ... *your* teeth. Sorry, baby brother, you got Mama's teeth ... I got Daddy's teeth. I jes' hope I didn't git his lungs.

Well, I'll never smoke another cig'rette as long as I live. See, that's where the Stupid side of the family really shows in you. You should try to quit, Jake. It's bad. I'm not tryin' to tell you how to run your life; jes' don't throw it down the toilet. Don't do like Daddy or like Bobby. You could be the first person in this family to finish high school, Jake. You know how much that'd mean to Mama? Jes' don't blow it is all I'm sayin'... Jes' don't blow it.

(Yawning.) Well, I'm gonna hit the hay. Don't forgit to turn out the light when you go to bed.

G'night, Jakey-Pooh.

Don't eat all that—It'll give you bad dreams.

Scene 4

(The following day. The diner. While SHE speaks with April, LYNNETTE is also writing checks and yelling

out orders to the kitchen.)

LYNNETTE. (*To the kitchen.*) Two eggs up—Spuds!
(*To April.*) Are fries extra on that special breakfast? (*Writing.*) Um-hmmmm.

My mama's tryin' to git me to go t'the prom, kin you beat that? I think it's the stupidest thing I ever heard. It's not even worth talkin' about.

There's a few minor considerations, like: no dress, no date, no diploma. I'm not givin' up—It jes' doesn't seem to make a whole lotta sense to act like I'm gonna go, is all.

(*To kitchen, suddenly.*) Put some piggies on that, please! Links! Thank you.

(*To April.*) Well it isn't anybody's fault, I think that's obvious. It jes' wasn't meant to be. No big deal.

Oh April, cut it out! I don't believe in sainthood, an' even if I did I wouldn't apply for the job. Well it jes' seems stupid to git all bent outta shape over what you can't have, or what you can't do or be. So, my daddy got sick an' I had to drop outta school! Big deal! I've heard lots worse.

What gits me is people who don't take advantage of what they've got—Like my sister, Katie. She plays dumb all the time to git boys, but all she's gittin' is dumb. I may be a hick, but someday I'm gonna git outta here—She'll still be dumb.

(*To unseen customer.*) You want more coffee? You sure?

(*Without moving her lips.*) April, can you cover my tables?—Bobby jes' walked in.

I love you, April.

(As Bobby approaches.)

Hi. Are you mad at me for not callin' you back las' night? I know it was your las' night home an' all, but I was busy at my house an' then I fell asleep.

I kinda wish you'd've left an' jes' written me in a couple of weeks from boot camp or somethin', cause no matter what I say, nothin's gonna change ... An' I can't blame you for wantin'to git outta this place—I think you could do a whole lot better than the army, but thinkin' hasn't gotten me anywheres yet.

It's always easier on a guy—"When the goin' gits tough, the guys git goin'." Least, that's how it looks from here.

I'm not mad at you, Bobby—I envy you. Your choices are so black an' white: stay or go. Sometimes I think girls don't git to make choices—They git pregnant, or they have to take care of someone else, or they spend their lives waitin' for somethin' that isn't comin'...

Well, I'm sorry, Bobby, but I can't promise to set around here an' wait for you. In the first place, I'll bet dollars to donuts you ain't comin' back, an' in the second place, even if you did, you'd be diff'rent—or I'd be diff'rent. You can't jes' put your life on hold—It's ... Oh, shoot, this is comin' out all wrong ...

Look, y'know in the cartoons when somebody runs off a cliff an' they jes' keep runnin', but they don't fall or nothin' bad happens to 'em 'til they look down? There's plenty of people in this town who've been runnin' in midair, an' they don't even notice this giant crack that's opened up underneath 'em, but they're fine jes' movin' their legs ... *(Ironically.)* You know me, though; I had to look down ...

Um, look—Don't say anything—Jes' git outta here before I start cryin' or somethin'. I'll see you around.

(HE is getting up and walking away.)

Hey, Bobby! You know what they say about the army, don'tcha? "It's not jes' a job; It's a blow job."

Scene 5

(Church interior.)

LYNNETTE. Thank you for seein' me, Reverend. I realize I haven't exactly been attendin' church on a regular basis, but I've been kinda busy these last five years ... Jes' kiddin'—No, um, actually, I've been under a lot of pressure lately an', um, I'm sure you'd tell me that if I was havin' some kinda trouble that church'd be the first place I should come to, so I did.

But, ah, this is gonna sound kinda weird, but, ah, part of my problem is church itself. More specifically ... Well, I don't know how else to say this, so I'll jes'... say it ... It's God; I don't believe in God anymore. An' I hope you don't take this personally, 'cause you're prob'ly settin' there thinkin', "Well why bother comin' all the way over here to tell me about it?", but that's jes' it; I still believe in you. An' I still believe in church for people who need somewhere to go to have somethin' to believe in.

An' I hope you'll pray for me, 'cause that way I'll

know someone is thinkin' about me. See, that's what I've always liked about prayin'; it's like people bein' together, or like, no, it's more like when people in diff'rent parts of the world look up at the same time an' see the same moon. It's somethin' that people can share. 'Cept when you pray, you're expressin' a wish. But someone on the other side of the world could be prayin' for the same thing ... Like maybe some girl in China, her daddy is sick, an' she's prayin' for him to git better. It's possible. So even if your prayers aren't answered, it's still kind of a comfort to know that you're sharin' somethin' with someone else. I can't explain it, but you know what I mean.

An' this way, if I'm wrong about God, at least I'll have all my bases covered.

Oh, an' if you could pray for my daddy too, I'd sure appreciate it.

Scene 6

(At the bank. LYNNETTE stands at the teller's window.)

LYNNETTE. Yeah, I want it all. My entire savin's account—Yes, that is correct. Of course you can; it's my money! Well, I want to withdraw it; all of it.

You don't seem to understand, I want to close the account.

No, no, it's got nothin' to do with the services here at the bank. It's none of your business what it's for, Bernice!

Alright, look ... How much money do I have to leave in the bank to keep the account open? Any amount at all?

Fine, give me everythin' I got saved up 'cept for one dollar.

I'm not interested in the interest!

Bernice, how would you like it if you ordered somethin' at the diner an' I wouldn't bring it to you because ... I don't know ... 'cause it was a flavor I didn't like! Like a strawberry shake! I don't like strawberrry at all—It tastes like Pepto Bismol! Well, I think it's gross, but people order it—All the time! Now how would you like it if you came into the diner jes' dyin' for a strawberry shake an' I wouldn't serve it to you on account of I don't like 'em? You *can't* ask April; you're settin' in *my* section!!

Look, it's not a trick question, I'm jes' tryin' to make a point here; the point bein' that chocolate's better'n strawberry.

Bernice, I appreciate your concern, but it *is* my money. An' if you're really worried about my savin' it for a rainy day, I got to tell you a little secret: From where I'm standin', it's rainin' cats an' dogs.

I'm not in any kinda trouble—No! Oh, Bernice—You are so sweet. Uh, I jes' really need the money for somethin' I been wantin' for a long time now. Don't worry, I know what I'm doin'.

Oh—Hey, listen; it's kind of a surprise, so I'd appreciate it if you didn't tell my mama jes' yet.

Thanks, Bernice.

Um, twenties will be fine.

Scene 7

(Car interior.)

LYNNETTE. ... Yup, that's my daddy; Frank Wilkes! You knew him at the plant, huh?

My name's Lynnette. Yeah, that's me; Frank an' Georgia's little girl.

You don't work at the plant anymore, do you? Well, if you did, you'd know that my daddy don't—He's got lung cancer. Yeah. He was diagnosed in January, so that's ... *(Counting.)* four months. He can't talk, 'cause it spread to his throat so he's supposed to stay home in bed an' drive Mama crazy. Well, she's workin' part time an' I've been workin' full time, so we've got things pretty well covered between us.

You think I look like my mama? ... Nah, I'll never be as pretty as her. She don't look a day over thirty, an' she's thirty-four! I'm seventeen. Yeah! Jake's sixteen, Katie's fourteen, Jimmy's eleven an' Candy's seven.

Now why would I make that up? That's my family! That's the real-est thing I ever knew!

How many kids do you have? Well, count yourself lucky; they're nothin' but trouble. I don't have any of my own, but my brothers an' sisters are enough. It's like they can't do anything for themselves ... They're not brain damaged or nothin'—They jes' act like it.

Katie's fourteen an' jes' discovered what boys are for; Jake's sixteen an' never even had a date! I know a lot of girls think he's cute, too. This girl I waitress with, April, she's crazy about him an' he don't even know she exists!

Maybe if he got his head out from under the car hood

an' stopped breathin' so many of them gas fumes he'd figure out what's what.

Sometimes I think boys can't see farther than their own noses ... Like, if they say they're gonna call you or somethin', they don't realize that you're gonna set an' wait by the phone. You might've even cancelled somethin' else jes' so's you'd be there when they called. An' then they don't understand when you git upset 'cause they didn't call. (*Laughing.*) I tell you, I don't know who's crazier: boys, or the girls runnin' after 'em! I guess if they set by the phone an' the guy doesn't call, they deserve to set there, an' if he *does* call, they deserve to *git* him!

You know that bumper sticker: "The more people I meet, the more I like my dog"? Oh man, sometimes I jes' git so fed up with people. An' you can git 'em to believe anything; I mean grown adults! I'm not talkin' about little kids; it's not their fault they're ignorant.

When we were kids, Ned Miller tol' me that if you swallowed a apple seed, a tree'd start growin' in your stomach an' the branches'd poke out through your ears while you were sleepin'... Then, you'd have to cut 'em back for the rest of your life. For years I looked at pregnant women an' figured they'd swallowed a watermelon seed ...

An' then in second grade when we had to sing "My Country 'Tis of Thee"; at the last part we used to sing ... "Land of the pilgrim's pride, land where our fathers fried, from every mountainside let freedom ring." So one time, before we even finished singin', Miz Clark jes' banged her fist down on the desk an' screamed, "This is not the land where our fathers FRIED!"... We didn't know the words were supposed to make sense ...

Am I talkin' too much?

I appreciate the lift. I hear a lot of people won't pick up hitchhikers anymore 'cause they think they're all axe murderers or somethin', but a lot of people stopped hitchin' 'cause they thought that the people who might pick 'em up could be rapists or somethin'. Actually, I wouldn't be hitchin' myself, but the car is broken an' Jake is still workin' on it.

I'm jes' goin' to visit my girlfriend in Amarillo. Yeah. She says she's got a real nice place there. She's married. I've never seen it—Her place, I mean.

Have you ever seen the ocean? That's somethin' I'd give my right arm for; for my daddy to git better an' to see the ocean.

Do you know the Jamesons? Faye's my age an' Bobby's nineteen an' they have a younger sister who's retarded.

Bobby went in the army yesterday. I'm not even sure how I feel about it yet. I've known Bobby my whole life, but now he's gone, it's weird, I can't really pitcher him outside of town at all. It's almost like he's a total stranger now. He's doin' an' seein' everything diff'rent ... When I try to pitcher where he's at or what he's doin', it's like I'm watchin' a movie.

The real challenge, I guess, would be to pitcher him standin' next to the ocean ... with Robert Redford. If it was a movie we could call it, "Robert an' Robert See the Sea." It sounds like a Easy Reader Book, don't it? ...

"See Robert. Robert sees the sea."

I would've named it "Butch Cassidy an' the Sundance Kid," but it's already been done. That's me an' April's favorite movie. We've seen it twelve times between us.

You wouldn't happen to know April, would you? Skinner? She works with me at the restaurant ... Got long, blonde hair; really curly. 'Course, she's not a natural blonde, but if you go in the restaurant don't stare at her like you're tryin' to figure it out, or nothin', 'cause she's very insecure, 'specially with guys, an' she'd prob'ly cry or somethin' if she knew you were lookin' to see if it was dyed. I mean, she prob'ly wouldn't break down an' cry in your corned beef hash or nothin', but she might go in the kitchen an' git upset for awhile, yeah. She's real pretty, too, but she acts like she don't know it when she's around guys.

I don't understand people who act diff'rent around people of the opposite sex. It's like, you shouldn't have to be married to someone for forty years to know what they're really like. An' everyone acts so nice an' polite to total strangers an' then they go home an' cuss out their wife or kick the dog or somethin'. Why can't people say what they really feel to the people they really love? What're they savin' it for?

I most always say what's on my mind. Mama says it's gonna git me in trouble someday, but I don't think so. I think what gits you in trouble is not sayin' ...

Now that my daddy lost his voice, I can tell there's a whole lot he wants to say.

If I ever git like that, I don't want to have any regrets. I'll jes' think to myself, "Well, Lynnette, you said it all. Put the past behind you an' git on with it."

When I was real small, my daddy came to pick me up from school one day ... I don't remember why. Maybe Jake was sick an' Mama was home with him ...

Anyway, Daddy an' me were walkin', an' this little cat

started to follow us, an' it was cryin' an' cryin', an' it was so cute I stopped to pick it up. While I was holdin' it, I noticed one of it's ears was sort of chewed up, like it'd been attacked by a bigger animal or somethin'.

I jes' felt so bad for this little cat I asked Daddy could we take it home, but he said, "Nunh-uh, honey, put it down." So of course when I did, it started cryin' again an' followin' me. Well, Daddy stopped walkin' an' got down on one knee an' looked me square in the eye an' said, "Lynnette honey, jes' don't look back." An' then he got up an' took my hand an' we walked away real fast.

It tore me up inside to leave that poor lil' thing behind, but what my daddy said has stayed with me to this day. It don't make sayin' goodbye any easier, but it helps you git on with it.

No sir, when I go I don't want to have nothin' saved up that I didn't spend or do or say. No regrets an' no lookin' back.

I better git out here. I don't have my friend's address, but I can call her an' she'll come pick me up. Anywhere along here is fine. Okay.

(LYNNETTE is getting out of the car.)

Listen, thanks again for the ride, an' I'm gonna tell my daddy I saw you. Okay, you take care now. It was real nice meetin' you ... 'Bye.

(Sound effect of a CAR pulling away, LYNNETTE smiling and waving. After a moment SHE looks around, then whirls as if to face an oncoming car. SHE sets her face in a determined expression and sticks out her thumb.)

Scene 8

(North Rim Lodge; Grand Canyon, Arizona. LYNNETTE is on the phone.)

LYNNETTE. April? Are you busy? Okay, listen, can you make me up a ham an' egg on a muffin an' deliver it ... to the Grand Canyon!! Yeah!! It's incredible! I'm fine, don't worry. I'm at this big lodge an' there's pitcher windows everywhere an' you kin jes' look right out an' see it! I haven't been to the bottom of the canyon; no. You kin take a donkey ride down there, but I can't afford it.

I'm hitchin', what do you think?

April, do I sound like someone who's bein' held at gunpoint?

What kind of sick-o's?

Well no one's even made a pass at me. Um-hmm; lucky me.

It's great! I've met a lot of really nice people. Well, one ride I got was a little weird; shell-shocked Vietnam vet havin' a sugar fit. He was eatin' Bit-O-Honey bars an' drinkin' Coke—Classic Coke—um-hmm—like he'd never stop. I swear, a six-pack of soda an' a whole bag of them Bit-O-Honey bite-sized miniatures ...

Well, now I'm with these three people who said they could give me a ride all the way to California ... Two guys an' a girl. An' a dog named Sasha ... In a van ...

It's great! Everythin's great! I wish you were here!

I know it's crazy, but I had to do it. When Bobby left I

realized I had to git outta there too. I don't want to stay home an' have babies an' git old an' die in Goodnight, Texas. An' I don't wanna go to the prom or be homecomin' queen.

An' I don't see why I have to take care of everyone else—Katie an' Jake are old enough. An' I truly despise waitressin' an' that money is not gonna make my daddy git better.

I talked to him the night Bobby left an' the next mornin' when I brung him up his breakfast, he give me a note. It said, "Lynnette—Go with my blessin'."

Don't start cryin'.

What? I can't understand what you're sayin'...

April? This is gittin' expensive, so quit cryin' on my bill.

C'mon, cut it out. I gotta hang up an' I can't if you're cryin' ...

Seriously, I can't afford this, so I'm gonna count to three an' then I'm gonna hang up, okay, April?

One ... Two ... Two-an'-a-half ... Three.

I'll try to call again.

Goodbye, April.

(SHE hangs up. A moment later, LYNNETTE grabs the phone and dials with a vengeance.)

Candy? How're you doin', sweetheart? It's your big sister Lynnette, silly; who'd you think it was? Papa Smurf? Honey, you been watchin' too much Saturday mornin' television. Lemme talk to Mama.

Well, who *is* there?

Lemme talk to him, then.

Jake? I'm at the Grand Canyon! Git Daddy on the phone; I wanna describe it to him.

I *know* he's in bed, stupid—Run upstairs to the hall phone an' see if the cord'll reach into Daddy's room.

Of course you should bother him!

Because I said so.

Jake, Daddy is dyin' of cancer; the last thing on his mind is smackin' you!

I am not makin' a joke out of it; for your information, he's my daddy, too. He knew I was gonna leave an' he gave me his blessin', so don't you DARE set there an' say that I turned my back on him—Don't you DARE!!

Where have *you* been all the time he's been sick—Out in the driveway with your head under the car; hidin'?

I had to quit school! *I* had to waitress at that stupid diner every day while you were hangin' out with your friends! *I* had to come home from work an' fix supper an' bring his food upstairs an' set there an' watch while he didn't eat it! Well, I didn't notice you ever volunteered. *I* had to wake up early to help Mama fix the lunches, make the breakfast an' git everyone off to school!

I did it for *him*—Who do you think I was doin' it for?

Jake, I didn't wanna be the one to go into his room one day an' find him dead. After everythin' I did for him, he's still gonna die.

He wanted me to go out an' make a life for myself. He wanted me to do the things he'll never git to do. He wants to know that the life he gave me will go on livin' after he's gone; not to waste it away in that town like he did ...

So don't try to make me hate myself for leavin', 'cause it was the toughest thing I've done yet. An' in a way, I did that for him, too. I thought about leavin', but he give me the strength to do it. He told me to go, an' I went, an' I can't apologize for that.

Now lemme speak to him. Yeah, I'll wait.

(There is a long pause as she does so.)

Hello? Daddy, is that you?

(LIGHTS fade.)

THE END

YOUR LIFE IS A FEATURE FILM

by Alan Minieri

118 OFF-OFF BROADWAY FESTIVAL PLAYS

Your Life is a Feature Film was originally produced in March, 1991 at the Sanford Meisner Theater in New York City by the Turnip Festival Company; Artistic Director, Joseph Massa. It was directed by Richard Hoetzel with the following cast:

LUKE .... Gregory Henderson

MOTHER .... Gloria Falzer

ROGER .... Ed Joseph

EDDIE .... Scott Fifer

JASMINE .... Erin Kelly

Stage Manager, Richard Keller

The Turnip Festival Company staged the same production for the Samuel French Festival at the Nat Horne Theater, June, 1992, with James Prendergast appearing in the role of ROGER and Richard Henning appearing in the role of EDDIE.

Your Life is a Feature Film received its West Coast premiere in November, 1991 at the West Coast Ensemble in Hollywood; Artistic Director, Les Hanson. It was directed by Bruce Grossberg with the following cast:

LUKE	Chad McCord
MOTHER	Nancy Hinman
ROGER	Michael Edelstein
EDDIE	Rudy Hynes
JASMINE	Lori Fox

Your Life is a Feature Film has received a 1991 *Drama-Logue* Award for Writing, and also an award in the Drury College National One-Act Playwriting Competition.

Men have always fought their misery with dreams. Although dreams were once powerful, they have been made puerile by the movies, radio and newspapers. Among many betrayals, this one is the worst.

Nathanael West,
Miss Lonelyhearts

CHARACTERS

LUKE: A young man
MOTHER: Luke's mother
ROGER: A film director
EDDIE: Roger's assistant
JASMINE: A young actress

SETTING

A New York City apartment shared by Luke and his mother.

AT RISE: In the room are a table and chairs, a couch, small bench or sideboard, and a television set. LUKE is finishing up packing his bags. His MOTHER enters carrying a cake with lighted candles on it, singing a birthday song. HE takes out his camera and snaps a picture of her. SHE places the cake on the table.

MOTHER. Twenty-one years old.
LUKE. Yeah. (*Pause.*) I'm sorry.
MOTHER. You do what you have to do.
LUKE. You'll be all right.
MOTHER. Oh, I know. I know.

(Pause.)

LUKE. Thanks for the cake.
MOTHER. Aren't you going to blow out your candles?
LUKE. I don't *have* to go. I don't have to do anything, I guess. But now the bags are packed. We have the tickets ...
MOTHER. I'll be fine, Luke. Make a wish.
LUKE. We'll come back. Who knows how long that series will last ...
MOTHER. I understand.
LUKE. But this is a big break for Regina, and I do have to go with her.
MOTHER. (*Pause.*) I know.
LUKE. I love her.
MOTHER. I know.

(Pause.)

LUKE. I don't know if I'm doing the right thing. I mean, I'm not going out there to *do* anything, really ...
MOTHER. Lucas ...
LUKE. But, I mean, well, I don't know what to do, but Barbet says that once I get my own studio out there ...
MOTHER. Luke ...
LUKE. And my own equipment ...
MOTHER. It's all right ...
LUKE. I'll have the freedom to—
MOTHER. Lucas. It's all right. We've been through all of this. We'll both do what we have to do. I only want what's best for you. Now make a wish and blow out your candles.
LUKE. *(Pause.)* Thank you.
MOTHER. Happy Birthday.

(LUKE blows out the candles and the room goes DARK. A MAN's voice yells out "Cut!", and the lights come on. ROGER, the director, is in the room with EDDIE, his assistant.)

ROGER. That's a take. *(To Mother.)* Beautiful, sweetheart.
LUKE. What ...? Who are you?
ROGER. How ya doin', Lucas, I'm Roger Crane. Pleasure to finally meet you.
LUKE. ... finally ...?
ROGER. Mark that one down, Eddie.
EDDIE. Got it.
LUKE. Mom, you know this guy?

ROGER. I think we have some explaining to do, Luke. (*To Mother.*) You were gorgeous, sweetheart, why don't you take five.

(*SHE lights up a cigarette.*)

LUKE. Mom ... you don't smoke ... (*To Roger.*) Who ... How did you get in here?
ROGER. Lucas, sit down.
LUKE. Excuse me?
ROGER. Come on, come on, come on, sit down. We should talk.
MOTHER. Go on ...
ROGER. You got those papers, Eddie?
EDDIE. Got 'em. (*EDDIE exits.*)
ROGER. Good. Come on now, Lucas, have a seat.
LUKE. Mom ... where is he going?
MOTHER. (*Referring him to Roger.*) Luke, please ...
LUKE. (*Sits cautiously.*) Do you know these guys?
MOTHER. Just listen to him.
ROGER. Lucas, my name is Roger Crane. Maybe you've heard of me ...?

(*LUKE looks at him blankly.*)

ROGER. No? Okay, well, that's all right, you've led a sheltered life.

(*ROGER laughs. EDDIE, from offstage, laughs too.*)

ROGER. No, no, no, seriously, Lucas, I'm a director. A film director. I'll assume you haven't heard of me because I haven't released a film in quite a while, and the reason for that is I am currently working on a long-term project. Very long-term. Twenty-one years to be exact.

(HE laughs. EDDIE too.)

ROGER. The situation we have here, Lucas—and I'll be direct because I'm a very direct person—but the situation is: Your life is a feature film.
LUKE. Excuse me?
ROGER. I know it's a bit of a shock, but what I'm telling you is we've been filming your entire life for the past twenty-one years and we intend to release it theatrically next Christmas.

(Pause.)

LUKE. Mom ...?

(HE turns to his MOTHER, who by now has transformed herself and is changing into less motherly clothes. LUKE moves away in shock at the sight of her.)

LUKE. I don't understand.
ROGER. Well, what it was was a concept I had way back—that the studio loved and locked into—to film a life as it really happens. The concept being that even a normal, mundane life can have meaning and ... drama, and ...

(EDDIE returns and speaks simultaneously with Roger.)

ROGER and EDDIE. ... box office potential.

ROGER. Now: Legal has informed us that we cannot release this film until you sign certain release papers—which my assistant, Eddie, currently has with him ... (*HE holds out his hand, EDDIE places the papers into it.*) ... and that you can sign these papers as of the moment you turned twenty-one years old. As you can see you will be very amply compensated for your work—a guaranteed back salary plus a percentage.[of the net. Sorry.] But, regardless, signing these papers will make you a wealthy man and allow us to release this film which we all believe very strongly in, et cetera, et cetera. Now:

(*ROGER pushes the papers toward LUKE, who pushes them away.*)

LUKE. Now, wait, wait, wait a second. Mom? Is this a joke or something? What's going on here? Mom?

MOTHER. Well, no, Luke, what he's saying is, you know, what it is. He's the director.

LUKE. I don't underst ...

ROGER. What I believe is confusing you, Lucas, is that your "mother" here is actually an actress. She did give birth to you, but it was in response to an audition notice in *Variety*. She's an actress. And I might add, a very capable actress. But, I mean, this is just a role for her.

LUKE. This is ...

ROGER. And I might add, the role of a lifetime. She's been an employed actress for the past twenty-one years. The woman has had ...

ROGER and EDDIE. ... more job security than Donahue, for chrissake.

LUKE. Now, wait, wait a minute. So everything she

says and does with me is acting?

ROGER. That's right.

LUKE. Mom ...?

MOTHER. I'm sorry, Lucas. And you can call me Candice if you want.

ROGER. The truth is, Luke, that everyone you've ever met or dealt with is an actor.

(Pause.)

LUKE. I don't believe you.

ROGER. You don't have to. It's true anyway.

LUKE. You mean like ... I don't know, Barbet?

ROGER. Yes. In the role of your boss the Famous Photographer—yes, that's right. An excellent character actor. I love that accent he does.

LUKE. That's fake?

ROGER. It's not fake. It's for the role.

LUKE. And all the guys I knew, let's say, in school, growing up ...

ROGER. Actors. Some parts bigger than others, of course, but you've never had any close friends anyway.

LUKE. Mr. Catalfumo ... Jerry, at the store ... Angie, at the temp agency ...

ROGER. All actors.

LUKE. Oh, come on, you expect me to believe that? Everybody?

ROGER. Yes.

LUKE. The guy at the newstand, the lady with the mole at Guiseppe's ... people on the street ...

ROGER. Extras.

LUKE. I don't believe this! This is ridiculous!

ROGER. It's all right here in black and white, Lucas. If you want I can get you a copy of the script.

LUKE. There's a script?

ROGER. Listen to this kid, "There's a script." Of course there's a script. What do you think I am ...

ROGER and EDDIE. ... Henry Jaglom?

LUKE. I never did anything from a script.

ROGER. Well, no, kid, of course not. We couldn't let you know it was scripted or it would have destroyed the gritty realism of the whole thing. But when you give everybody around you a script, we're pretty much able to determine where the action's going to go.

LUKE. How did you get in here, anyway?

ROGER. Kid—

LUKE. How could you have filmed my whole life without me noticing it?

ROGER. It's the magic of the movies, kid. With a big enough budget we can do anything.

LUKE. Mom, is this guy ...? This is, this is a little ... uh ... I'm, I'm leaving. I'm going over to Regina's. (*HE heads for the door.*)

ROGER. Whoa, whoa, whoa, now, kid. Of course you're going over to Regina's, but first we have contracts to take care of ...

LUKE. I'm not signing anything.

ROGER. Now, now, I understand. You're upset. It's perfectly natural. Go get Lucas a Coke, Eddie. Or, no, Pepsi. He likes Pepsi.

(*EDDIE exits.*)

LUKE. How do you know?

ROGER. (*Laughs.*) Kid. I'm the director. What do you think, that preferring Pepsi over Coke is genetic? Your personal choice? We planned it, it's in the script. [The truth is it's a promotional thing. I hate it too, but somebody's gotta cover costs.]
LUKE. I have to go now.
ROGER. Now, now, now, please ...

(EDDIE returns with the Pepsi, blocking Luke's exit.)

ROGER. Here. Drink your Pepsi. Relax, heh?
LUKE. I really have to—
ROGER. No, now, you don't *have* to do anything. Come on. We're going to sit and discuss this like civilized human beings.
MOTHER. Am I done yet, Roger?
ROGER. You want to go, sweetheart?
MOTHER. I have auditions.
ROGER. Could you hang around a while longer?
MOTHER. Well, if you need me ...
LUKE. ... you have auditions ...?
ROGER. We might, baby. Could you do it? Just to see.
MOTHER. (*Sighs.*) If you *really* need me.
ROGER. You're a doll. I love you. I love this woman.
LUKE. Mom, what are you auditioning for?
MOTHER. Could he stop calling me "mom," please?
ROGER. Kid, I'm gonna have to ask—
LUKE. Mom ...
MOTHER. Roger!
ROGER. All right! All right. Please. Everyone just relax, all right? Kid: Don't call her mom, okay? Not when the cameras are off. And Candy—lighten up a little, heh?

MOTHER. I'm tense.

ROGER. I know ...

MOTHER. This will be the first time in a long while I'm going to be out of work, Roger, and I'm tense.

ROGER. I know. I know. It'll be hard for all of us to get used to.

LUKE. What ...? Why will she be out of work?

ROGER. Well ...

LUKE. She's not going to be my mother anymore?

ROGER. Well, technically I suppose she'll always be that. But after today she won't be playing the *role* of your mother anymore.

MOTHER. I don't know *what* I'm going to do.

LUKE. (*To Roger.*) Why not?

ROGER. (*Pause.*) This is the tricky part, kid, it really is. I said this would be the tricky part, didn't I, Eddie?

EDDIE. (*Eating a sandwich.*) Oh, you said: "This will be the tricky part."

ROGER. The thing is, kid ... well ... we plan on shooting the last scene today.

LUKE. The last scene ...?

ROGER. The ... well, what it is is in the last scene ... you die.

(*Pause.*)

LUKE. I die.

ROGER. Yes, the movie is a tragedy.

LUKE. So, I have to act out a death scene?

ROGER. No, uh, actually you just die.

(*Pause. LUKE starts to laugh.*)

LUKE. Get outta here.
ROGER. No, it's true.
LUKE. You're kidding me, right?
ROGER. Kid, we're shooting a true story here. All true stories end in death. Whathisname said that. Who was it, Eddie?
EDDIE. Hemingway.
ROGER. Hemingway. Another great artist. Thank you.
EDDIE. Check.
ROGER. Your life is a true story, therefore you must die.
LUKE. Well, sure, okay, but it doesn't have to be now. I mean, why not sixty years from now?
ROGER. Well, think about it, what's more tragic, an old man dying or a young healthy kid on the brink of a new life. (*Beat*.) And I'll admit it, okay, costs are a factor. The longer we wait the higher the tab. [We're already over budget.]
LUKE. So, wait, now, you want me to sign over to you the right to kill me and film it?
ROGER. That's a very harsh way of phrasing it.
LUKE. Why would I agree to my own death?
ROGER. Hey, kid, what do you think that if you don't sign, you'll never die? At least this way you'll go out a star.
LUKE. Mom—or, or, whoever you are—you agreed to this? You would let them take my life for a movie?
ROGER. It's not just another movie, kid.
LUKE. (*To Roger*.) Please ...
MOTHER. I'm sorry, Luke, I have a contract.
LUKE. But you agreed to it? Right from the start you

said, "Okay, I'll bring this person into the world and he'll only exist to be a part of this production?" Because that's what you're telling me.

ROGER. Hey, kid, I know actors who'd kill for this part.

LUKE. Shut up! (*To Mother.*) I want *you* to tell me it's true. That you agreed to all this beforehand.

ROGER. Eddie has a copy of her contract right here, kid.

(EDDIE hands the contract to LUKE.)

MOTHER. It's true, Luke, I'm sorry. I needed the work.

LUKE. (*Looking over the contract.*) Everything you've ever said to me is a lie.

MOTHER. It's not lying, Lucas, it's ... Jesus. Roger? It's acting, Luke. It's a job. There's a script ... It becomes real to me when it happens, but when the scene is over, I'm me again. An actor shouldn't get too attached to her role.

LUKE. I can't believe it ...

MOTHER. Roger, I'm getting such a headache.

ROGER. Eddie, go get her some aspirin.

(EDDIE exits.)

LUKE. I can't believe I couldn't tell.

ROGER. I only work with best actors, kid. Casting is everything.

LUKE. (*To Mother.*) And who's my father?

MOTHER. Your father?

LUKE. Yes. Apparently I was conceived for the sole purpose of this movie. You told me he died before I was born.

MOTHER. That's what was in the script.

LUKE. Godammit, I don't care about the script! Who is he?

(Pause.)

MOTHER. He is.

LUKE. You …?

ROGER. Well, technically, I suppose, but I think of this whole project as my baby.

LUKE. You ...?

ROGER. Hey, somebody had to get the ball rolling. Seems like only yesterday, Candy, doesn't it?

(EDDIE brings aspirin for Candy.)

LUKE. And now you're willing to sacrifice your own son for ... for ... box-office receipts?

ROGER. Hey! Hey, wait a second. I am a serious filmmaker. My name will be passed on not by my children, but by my work. This film will be my legacy! My lasting and selfless contribution to this world in which we live. I insist that you do not belittle it.

(Pause.)

LUKE. Okay, I won't belittle it. I also won't let you release it.

ROGER. Now wait a second, kid ...

LUKE. No, it's pretty simple actually. I mean, what's so hard about this? I don't agree to anything that takes my life as the price. Case closed. Goodbye.

ROGER. I understand. Honestly I do ...

LUKE. (*Gathering his bags.*) I'm going to get Regina and we're going to go out to California. She'll have her role in that series, I'll start up my photography studio and everything will be fine.

ROGER. Kid, uh ...

LUKE. No, that's it. The only hang-up I had was leaving *you* behind by yourself. But now ... I don't really care. You're not who I thought you were. (*HE starts to exit.*)

ROGER. Eddie, we might have to juggle locations. Call in Regina, willya?

EDDIE. Check.

(*LUKE stops. EDDIE exits.*)

ROGER. (*Calling after Eddie.*) And set up for those dailies I told you about.

LUKE. Regina's not in on this.

ROGER. Everybody's in on it, kid.

LUKE. No. No, I don't believe that.

ROGER. Her name's Jasmine O'Connor, kid. I can still remember when I first saw her headshot. Must be two years now. I took one look and I said—that's the one.

LUKE. No, I'm sorry, I think you're the one that's been fooled this time.

ROGER. Kid, listen ...

LUKE. No, really, I mean, we're in ... we're in love, her and me. I *know* that. That's the only thing I'm certain of.

ROGER. Okay, kid, whatever you say. We'll talk when she gets here.

(Pause.)

LUKE. I mean, even if she started out playing it as a role ... Now ... now it's the real thing.
ROGER. Okay. Fine.
LUKE. You'll see.
ROGER. Sure. Hey, maybe you're right. Stranger things have happened.

(Pause.)

LUKE. Oh, God.

(Pause.)

ROGER. Hey, but, kid, you should see the dailies we've had. I mean for the most part—garbage. But on the good days there's been stuff that's made us all proud. You growing up, becoming a man ... Simple, but really powerful.

(ROGER leads LUKE back to the table. The MOTHER joins them.)

ROGER. Hey, remember back in high school when you were still living in Jersey and you brought the food over to that teacher of yours house. The one you said before ... Mr. Catalfumo.

You stole the stuff from that gourmet shop you delivered for—working for Jerry. The Adirondack House.

It was when Catalfumo had just gotten fired. He was living in that dilapidated little green and white house on Grove Street. With the broken step up to the porch.

And when you got there he was drunk. As usual.

He was sitting alone in that dark little kitchen ...

And you came up to him ...

And you handed him the bag ...

And he beat you with a stick.

(Pause.)

LUKE. I remember.

ROGER. And then he called the police on you. He told them you broke in and he had to defend himself. And they brought you home to your mother, and you were so ashamed. But you couldn't tell her the truth, that old guy had been like a father to you. You held it all inside and you were bruised and you hurt all over ...

LUKE. And that night I cried in my mother's arms.

ROGER. That's right.

LUKE. I thought I was all grown up after that. That I knew all there was to know. That was the last time I ever did that, cried in your arms.

MOTHER. Yes.

LUKE. You remember it?

MOTHER. Sure. It was a good scene.

ROGER. You see, Luke, now the whole world will be able to see it from your perspective. You've had to keep the truth to yourself, but now, because it's on film, everyone will see that you were just trying to do good.

You didn't deserve to be beaten and humiliated and fired from your job. Now you have a chance to tell everyone your story. A story where you're the hero.

LUKE. I guess so. (*Pause.*) I remember the first time I saw Regina.

ROGER. That'll be in there. It'll all be in there.

LUKE. We both had temp assignments at the same company, and right from the start it was like we had our own little world. Our inside joke about how everything was so crazy and only we knew it .... Right from the start. (*Beat.*) I bet that was kind of a cute scene, huh?

ROGER. Absolutely. Touching, really. Hey, and how about the time I got you your first camera?

LUKE. Huh? ... you?

ROGER. Sure. I always knew you'd have knack for it.

LUKE. (*Laughs.*) No, I've always been a lousy photographer. I hardly even like it that much. It's a stupid thing to do, trying to ... stop time, control a moment .... But I didn't want to bother with college or nine-to-five or any of that ...

ROGER. I know.

LUKE. And I had that camera and I figured it was something.

ROGER. Which was exactly what happened with me when I left high school.

LUKE. Really?

ROGER. Yes. Mine was a movie camera, but yes.

LUKE. Wow.

ROGER. And now everyone will see our story. Everyone will understand.

(*Pause.*)

LUKE. How am I supposed to die?
ROGER. Die?
LUKE. Yes, I assume that it's in the script.
ROGER. Well, uh, actually, yes. It is.

(Pause.)

LUKE. And?
ROGER. I don't know ... I guess you do have to know eventually, though. What happens is, uh, Regina does it.
LUKE. Does what?
ROGER. She kills you.
LUKE. Regina?
ROGER. Yes.
LUKE. No.
ROGER. Yes.
LUKE. Why?
ROGER. She thinks you betrayed her.
LUKE. Why would she think that?
MOTHER. I told her you did.
LUKE. *You* told her?
MOTHER. Yes. The mother.
LUKE. Told her what?
MOTHER. That you were unfaithful. That you've been deceiving her and having an affair with that Maureen. That model Barbet uses.
LUKE. Why did you tell her that?
MOTHER. You mean what was my motivation?
LUKE. Yes! No ... Why did you tell her that?
MOTHER. Well, I don't want you to leave with her. I want you to stay here with me.

LUKE. But you said you understood.

MOTHER. I do but I still don't want you to go. The thing is I have no real friends in this city, I wouldn't have even moved in if it wasn't for you. I hate my work, I have no relatives, no men in my life, no nothing really except for you. I don't want to have to find a different life and that's what'll have to happen if you leave.

LUKE. So you tried to destroy the one thing in my life that means anything to me?

MOTHER. Well she doesn't look at it as destroying.

LUKE. Who's "she"?

MOTHER. The character. Or "me," I mean, whoever, I don't look at it as destroying. I look at it as the best thing for both of us.

LUKE. How could that be?

MOTHER. Well, you're going out there to a strange place, and I figure Regina's going to dump you once her career as an actress gets going out there ... And ... what else, that you'll never make it on your own as a photographer without my support, and, you know, stuff like that.

LUKE. But none of that's true.

MOTHER. Well she thinks it is. She's justifying her own selfishness, but she's familiar with loneliness and she doesn't want to—

LUKE. And, wait, Regina believed this story?

MOTHER. At first no, because she knew that I didn't want you to go and that I was probably just sabotaging the relationship. But then—and this is where it's so well-written—then I admitted to her that, yes, I want you to stay here in New York, of course I do. But I'm telling her this because I know that you're just using her for her connections and the money she'll have, and that things like this always end in heartache for everyone et cetera. And eventually I'm able to sway her and convince her that your love for her isn't real and she's totally crushed. I leave knowing that she'll never believe a word you say and will tell you she won't want you to come with her.

ROGER. It was a marvelous scene. We shot it last week.

MOTHER. The thing is I have no idea she'd go so far as to kill you, but I really end up bringing it about. I end up ruining all three of our lives because I love you so much. It's chilling stuff.

ROGER. Wonderful stuff.

MOTHER. And so well-written. It's so hard to find good scripts. I don't know what I'm going to do now, Roger. Especially if this film doesn't get released.

ROGER. (*Pause. ROGER comes to Luke.*)

Kid, listen. If you don't sign, who are you? You're a nobody. A non-person. You have no family, no friends, no genuine past, no hope for the future—

LUKE. I have Regina.

ROGER. I told you, kid—

LUKE. I know what you told me, I don't believe you! Regina is not in on this. She's not going to kill me![**]

(*EDDIE enters with videotapes that HE brings to the VCR.*)

ROGER. Ah, perfect, Eddie.
LUKE. What is *this*?
ROGER. It's from last week.
MOTHER. Oh, good, I love to watch dailies.

[**]See page 155

ROGER. Eddie, where's my cigar?

(The tape plays. On screen, LUKE and REGINA are in bed. REGINA is climaxing.)

ROGER. Whoa, whoa, cut, cut. Eddie, I said the park scene.

(EDDIE quickly changes the tapes.)

LUKE. That was Regina and me!
ROGER. I know, I know ...
LUKE. How did you get in there?
ROGER. Kid, listen ...
LUKE. She was acting?
ROGER. Listen, listen, just relax, all right? It's the romantic angle. We gotta give the people what they want.
LUKE. Oh, God ...
EDDIE. Sorry. *(EDDIE gets the correct tape going. On screen, LUKE and REGINA are romping in the park.)*
LUKE. ... I don't want to watch anymore.
ROGER. I hate to do it kid, but it's for your own good. I want you to be prepared for the reality of the situation, here. *(To Mother.)* The camera loves her doesn't it?
MOTHER. Yes. It does.
LUKE. *(Realizing something.)* Wait a second ... *(HE goes to the VCR and fast-forwards.)*
ROGER. Careful, kid, that's studio property.
LUKE. Shhh. *(HE turns up the sound. On screen, LUKE and REGINA are toasting with cans of Pepsi.)*
JASMINE. Here's to us. *(THEY drink.)* You know, Luke, I'll always love you.

LUKE. (*On screen.*) I know.
ROGER. Kid, what are you—
LUKE. (*On stage.*) Shhh!
JASMINE. No, I mean, you never know what might happen out there ...
LUKE. (*On screen.*) Regina ...
JASMINE. Hollywood changes people.
LUKE. (*On screen.*) What are you talking about?
JASMINE. People do things that you probably never even imagined.
ROGER. Eddie, is this in the script?
EDDIE. I'd have to check.
LUKE. (*On screen.*) You don't have to worry about that.
JASMINE. Because even if things happen that you can't understand, or maybe seem so strange that they can't even be real—I'll still love you.
LUKE. (*On screen.*) I know.
JASMINE. No matter what.
LUKE. (*On screen.*) Yeah, okay.
ROGER. Shut it off, Eddie. That scene's too goddam long.

(*EDDIE shuts it off and exits.*)

LUKE. You heard that didn't you?
ROGER. Yes, kid ...
LUKE. You *are* the one that's been fooled!
ROGER. Relax, heh.
LUKE. That wasn't in any script.
ROGER. So she improvised. I think it works.
LUKE. We *are* going to escape. The two of us.

MOTHER. Roger. She better not be planning to run away with him.
ROGER. I know, sweetheart.
MOTHER. I mean you don't really think ...
ROGER. Jasmine's got a mind of her own.
LUKE. That's right she does.
MOTHER. I never trusted that girl.
EDDIE. (*Enters.*) She's here.

(*JASMINE enters.*)

LUKE. Regina? (*Pause.*) Regina tell them all the truth. Tell that we really are in love and that we can walk away from all this. Go on tell them.
JASMINE. (*Pause. JASMINE looks to Roger.*) Is he serious?
LUKE. Oh, God ...
JASMINE. No, I mean ... Is he?
ROGER. Uh, Jas ...
JASMINE. Eddie told me you told him, Roger. (*To Eddie.*) That's what you told me.
EDDIE. We did.
ROGER. We did, Jas.
JASMINE. Oh. Well then what's with him? (*SHE goes to Roger.*) How you doing, babe? (*SHE kisses Roger and pats him on the rump. SHE goes over to CANDICE, on the couch.*) Hi, Candy, how are you?
MOTHER. Oh, God. Fine, I suppose.
JASMINE. Still nothing, huh?

(*The MOTHER shakes her head.*)

LUKE. Regina! (*HE looks desperately to Jasmine. Pause.*)

JASMINE. Roger. I mean, come on, what's up with this? Don't you have things under control?

ROGER. We do, sweetheart, it's just some minor details ...

JASMINE. All right then. It's bad enough we're switching locations.

MOTHER. (*Flipping through a* Variety *that she had hidden under the couch seat cushions.*) You have any luck?

JASMINE. I got a call-back for that guest spot I told you about ...

(*CANDICE crushes her* Variety.)

JASMINE. ... but I don't really care about it.
MOTHER. Oh, God ...
JASMINE. No, I'll just relax for a while. I mean, I need a break. Don't you?

(*The MOTHER starts to cry.*)

JASMINE. Oh, now, Candy ... (*JASMINE comforts her.*)

MOTHER. I need a job is what I need! I didn't prepare for this!

JASMINE. Oh, come on, sweetheart ...
ROGER. Eddie, go get some Pepsi.

(*EDDIE exits.*)

MOTHER. I didn't save, I didn't invest ... I don't know what I'm going to do!

JASMINE. It'll be all right ...

ROGER. I'll make some calls for you ...

CANDICE. This role has been so damn demanding. Twenty-one years of ... My personal life is terrible! It's non-existent!

JASMINE. Candice, listen to me. You're a strong, talented woman. It's not easy but you'll find work. And once this film is released you'll have all kinds of offers. I mean, that's what I'm counting on.

LUKE. Who are you?

JASMINE. Excuse me?

LUKE. I said who are you? I don't know who you are.

JASMINE. Oh, I'm sorry. I'm Jasmine. I've been playing Regina.

LUKE. So you're not going to California with me.

JASMINE. To ...? Roger?

LUKE. You don't have a part in a television series out there.

JASMINE. Ha. I wish.

(The MOTHER sobs.)

ROGER. Eddie! Where's that Pepsi?

(EDDIE enters with a large bottle of Pepsi and a cup of soda for Candice. HE sets the bottle on the sideboard and brings the cup to Candice.)

JASMINE. Oh, Candy ...
LUKE. I really thought you loved me.

JASMINE. Really. Well, then maybe I'm a better actress than I thought.

(SHE laughs. ROGER joins in. EDDIE, too.)

ROGER. The truth is that both of my girls are wonderful actresses. I'm the luckiest director around.

LUKE. I loved you.

JASMINE. Well, that's ... That's, uh ... Roger, what's going on?

LUKE. *(Coming toward her.)* You lied to me. You've been lying to me since I met you.

JASMINE. Roger ...?

ROGER. Kid ...

LUKE. You helped set it all up. You were in on this whole thing against me and you knew it from the beginning!

JASMINE. I'm not against you.

LUKE. You're a part of the production. You're going to kill me.

JASMINE. It's in the script.

LUKE. I don't care about the script! You can make your own choices!

JASMINE. I have a contract!

LUKE. Oh, fuck the contract! Everybody's got a contract. Like that justifies anything you do. That if I sign this goddam contract then you can do whatever you want to me and it's all fine.

JASMINE. He hasn't signed it yet?

ROGER. I checked it out with legal, kid. It'll stand up in any court.

LUKE. Oh, shut up.

JASMINE. Without the contract, Rog, it's murder.

ROGER. It's a unique situation we all admit—it's taken forever with the paperwork, kid—but the contract allows—

LUKE. Shut up with the contract! I'm sick of contracts. They don't mean anything to me.

ROGER. Oh, they don't?

LUKE. No.

ROGER. Well, then you know what? You're a brat. What do you think society is? It's contracts ... Agreements.

MOTHER. What happens when the contracts run out, though? What happens then?

ROGER. You're not helping the situation, sweetheart.

LUKE. I never agreed to anything about this movie. I never signed a goddam thing.

ROGER. Yes, but agreements were made on the coast before you were even born. This is the world you were brought into and you have an obligation to it. We all do, right on down to Eddie. Look at Eddie, working to make this happen. Why can't you be more like Eddie?

MOTHER. More professional.

ROGER. That's right. You're an adult now, young man. Don't be irresponsible. (*Pause.*) Eddie get the contract.

LUKE. (*Grabs Jasimine.*) Come on we're getting out of here.

JASMINE. Let go of me!

LUKE. I said come on!

JASMINE. Roger!

ROGER. Kid ...

LUKE. (*Dragging Regina out, grabbing his bags, etc.*)

Regina, I love you—or Jasmine, or whoever you are. We're getting out of here ...
 JASMINE. (*Struggling against him.*) Oh, please—
 LUKE. We're going to start a life away from all these contracts and agreements and people ... We'll escape from all this—
 JASMINE. Roger!

(LUKE grabs her as SHE tries to pull away and HE kisses her forcibly. Finally, SHE pushes him away violently and breaks free. LUKE crashes into the table, his hands going into his birthday cake. Pause.)

 LUKE. You can bring me that contract, Eddie.

(EDDIE gives him a towel to wipe his hands and places the contract before him. LUKE looks it over.)

 LUKE. You got a pen?
 EDDIE. (*Feeling his pockets.*) Um ...
 ROGER. You don't have a pen? Get him a goddam pen.

(HE locates a pen and gives it to LUKE. LUKE signs the contract. ROGER takes it and hands it to EDDIE.)

 ROGER. Congratulations, kid. You're rich and successful. All right, let's get it ready. You better come fix yourself up, Candy.

(EDDIE, ROGER and the MOTHER exit. After a moment JASMINE goes to Luke.)

JASMINE. Get out of here.

LUKE. What?

JASMINE. (*Dragging him out.*) I said get out of here. Come on.

LUKE. What are you doing?

JASMINE. I'm giving you your chance to escape ...

LUKE. Now, wait, wait ...

JASMINE. Luke, don't you realize what—Just go. Now.

LUKE. But ...

JASMINE. Please, I don't want to have to—

LUKE. But why? Why are you doing this?

JASMINE. Why do you think? Are you that naive? I love you. I couldn't say that in front of ... but ... Just go.

LUKE. So then you really ...

JASMINE. Luke, don't ...

LUKE. You really *do* ...? When you said no matter what, you really meant it?

JASMINE. Luke, there's no time for this. Go. Please.

LUKE. (*HE stops.*) But I can't go without you.

JASMINE. You don't need me.

LUKE. But I do, I do ...

JASMINE. Why? Why can't you just go out on your own?

LUKE. Because there's nowhere to go.

JASMINE. Here, take your bags. You have your camera, you'll find something. Anything.

LUKE. But not without you!

JASMINE. Luke ...

LUKE. Don't you see? There's nothing for me out there. There never has been.

JASMINE. Luke, that's not true.
LUKE. Yes it is. I know that now.
JASMINE. But, Luke, we both have to survive ...
LUKE. But I'd have to deceive myself to survive and I don't want to do that. At least with us we can escape from all that.
JASMINE. Luke ... I can't just walk away from all this ...
LUKE. How many times have we said to each other that none of that other stuff matters? We don't need all that, but we do need each other so that we know that something is real. So even if we can't trust anyone else, at least we can trust and have faith in each other. You said you'd always love me no matter what because you know that love always survives. It's the only thing that does. It's the only thing left to believe in. (*HE kisses her. SHE succumbs.*) I know it'll be hard for you because I'll be an outcast.
JASMINE. Then I guess we'll be outcasts together.
LUKE. That's right.

(*Pause.*)

JASMINE. Then I guess we should go together.
LUKE. (*Embraces her.*) I knew it ...
JASMINE. I mean, I wouldn't be able to stand it knowing you're out there ... being an outcast without me. Eventually I'd have to go out and find you.
LUKE. (*Kissing her.*) I love you.
JASMINE. I love you too. (*THEY kiss.*) Hey ... (*SHE pours two Pepsis, hands him one.*) Here's to us.

(THEY toast. HE downs his glass.)

LUKE. Now, come on. Let's get out of here.

(HE gathers his bags and starts to the door. SHE remains still.)

JASMINE. Are you sure you're ready to leave her behind?
LUKE. What? My mother? I don't understand.

(Pause. SHE doesn't move. HE starts toward her.)

LUKE. Regina, let's go, I—*(HE buckles suddenly from pain in his stomach.)* Oh, God. *(HE drops to the floor.)* Regina ...
JASMINE. Liar. Dirty filthy liar.
LUKE. Regina ...
JASMINE. Standing there and talking to me about trust ... I trusted you! But you're not who I thought you were, are you? You're a goddam filthy liar is what you are!
LUKE. I ...
JASMINE. I *did* put all my faith in you, but you betrayed me. Pretending you were afraid to leave because of your mother but it was actually because of that other *slut*!
LUKE. Regina, I ...
JASMINE. Don't try to deny it you bastard. She told me everything. You destroyed me. Everything I believed, all my trust, destroyed. *You've* poisoned *me*. You *made* me do this, I didn't want to. I even gave you a chance to escape, I told you to go, why didn't you? Did you think I

would just sit back and let this sort of thing happen to me? That I would ignore the truth and still run away with you? Don't you know me better than that? Don't you know?

(LUKE is dead. SHE cries over his body.)

JASMINE. You stupid son-of-a-bitch. Don't you know anything? (*SHE holds his dead body in her arms.*)
ROGER. (*From off.*) Cut!

(ROGER comes on. JASMINE abruptly stops crying.)

JASMINE. Oh, that was a tough scene.
EDDIE. (*Entering.*) That's a wrap.
ROGER. Beautiful, sweetheart. Captured on film for all posterity.
JASMINE. Thanks. We still on for dinner?
ROGER. You know it.

(SHE pats him on the rump and starts out, passing the MOTHER who is on her way in.)

JASMINE. Gotta run, Candy. We'll talk.
MOTHER. Sure.

(JASMINE exits. ROGER follows her out.)

ROGER. Beautiful. Just beautiful.
MOTHER. I don't know what I'm going to do now.

(SHE sits. EDDIE surveys the room, gathers his things. HE takes a taste of the cake and whistles a birthday

tune as HE exits. The LIGHTS fade out.)

END OF PLAY

AUTHOR'S NOTE

For those who do not have the technical means to do the video scene, the following scene may be substituted at that point:

ROGER. Eddie! (*EDDIE enters.*) I think we may need to see some dailies, Eddie.
EDDIE. Check.
LUKE. I don't care about any dailies.
ROGER. Maybe from the park scene last week. Or maybe that candlelight dinner scene. (*To Luke.*) You'll love that one.
LUKE. (*Recalling something.*) Wait a second ... She warned me about this.
ROGER. Who did?
LUKE. Regina. At dinner. The candlelight dinner.
ROGER. Yes, a very pretty shot. The lighting was crucial. Go ahead, Eddie.
LUKE. No, she said to me: "No matter what happens, Luke—I'll always love you."
ROGER. Yes, very romantic, I know.
LUKE. (*Still recalling.*) "Even if things happen that you can't understand, or maybe seem so strange that they can't even be real, remember: I'll still love you."
ROGER. (*Pause.*) She said that?
LUKE. And then we toasted. "Here's to us," she said. "No matter what."
ROGER. Eddie, is that in the script?
EDDIE. I'd have to check.
MOTHER. Roger, what's going on?
ROGER. Nothing, sweetheart. The kid's upset. He's

delirious.
LUKE. At the time I didn't know, but she was warning me ...
ROGER. Or maybe she improvised. I think it works within the context of—
LUKE. You *are* the one that's been fooled.
ROGER. Relax, heh.
LUKE. We *are* going to escape, the two of us.
MOTHER. Roger. She better not be planning to run away with him.
ROGER. I know, sweetheart ...
MOTHER. I mean, you don't really think ...
ROGER. Jasmine does have a mind of her own sometimes.
LUKE. That's right, she does.
MOTHER. I never trusted that girl.

(A KNOCK comes on the door.)

EDDIE. She's here.

The play continues with JASMINE's entrance.
If this version is used, ROGER's line on page 135, "And set up for those dailies I told you about," must also be cut.

The original New York production did the video scene by using a video monitor on stage. The West Coast production did the same scene by using recorded sound and the television facing away from the audience. For the Samuel French Festival, due to technical and time limitations, this revised version was used. Each way works, but the video monitor on stage is ideal because it allows the audience to *see* Jasmine as Regina and her loving relationship with Luke, increasing the impact of her subsequent betrayal.

COSTUME PLOT

Luke: Light blue turtleneck, pants, jacket or overcoat

Mother: Dress with apron, slipper,s black slip, red bolero jacket, short black skirt, black fishnet stockings, heels

Roger: Button down shirt, dark slacks, dark blazer

Eddie: T-shirt, jeans, baseball cap

Jasmine: White blouse, green button-down sweater, jeans

PROPERTY PLOT

Luke's bags
Camera (Luke)
Birthday cake with candles
Plastic forks, knives, napkins
Cigarettes and lighter (Mother)
Two contracts (Eddie)
Can of Pepsi
Sandwich (Eddie)
Jasmine's headshot (Eddie)
Aspirins
Variety magazine
Bottle of Pepsi
Cups
Pen (Eddie)
Towel (Eddie)

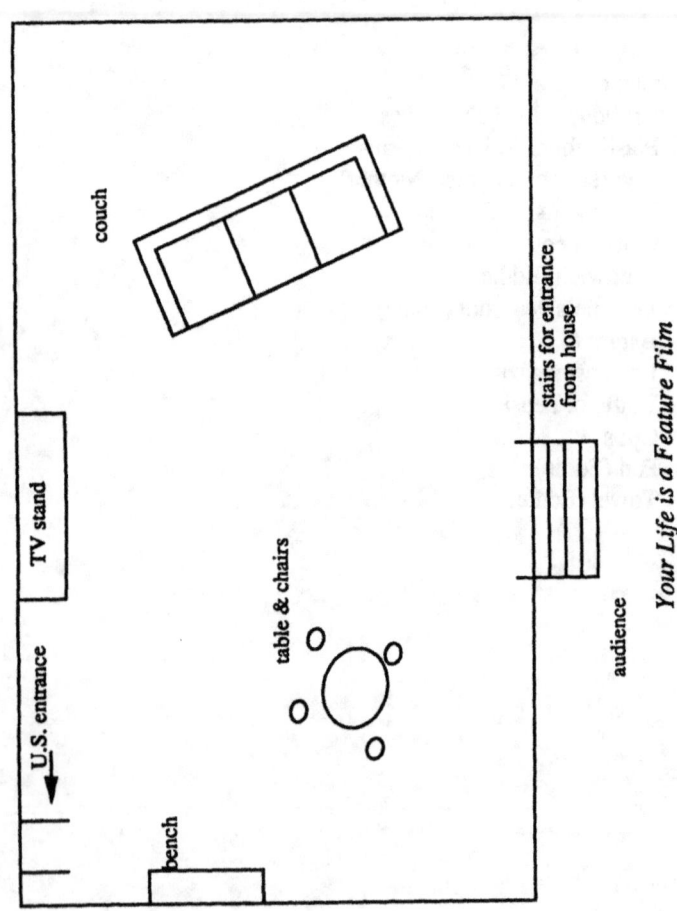

www.ingramcontent.com/pod-product-compliance
Lightning Source LLC
Chambersburg PA
CBHW072006290426
44109CB00018B/2150